Stepping Up

2ND INNING

TO THE PLATE

More Inspiring Interviews with Major Leaguers

Stepping Up

2ND INNING

TO THE PLATE

by David Kloser

Stepping Up To The Plate

Published by:
Capucia, LLC
211 Pauline Drive #513
York, PA 17402
www.capuciapublishing.com

ISBN: 978-1-945252-64-8
Library of Congress Control Number: 2019907802

Cover Design: Michael Bernier
Layout: Andrea Reider

Printed in the United States of America

Attention: Schools, Baseball Camps and Businesses

Books are available at quantity dis-counts with bulk purchase for education, business, or sales promotional use. For information, please contact:

Capucia LLC
211 Pauline Drive #513, York, PA 17402
Ph: (800) 930-3713
www.capuciapublishing.com

Contents

To anyone who has had the courage to step up to the plate and go after their dreams.

Acknowledgments

A book like this could not be done alone. I had a team helping me, whether they knew it or not. So, I want to acknowledge all those people who supported, encouraged and allowed me the space to make my dreams come true.

Thank you to all the Major League teams for allowing me access to your clubhouses and players, specifically: Jay Alves, Jim Anderson, Brian Bartow, John Blake, Rob Butcher, Richard Cerrone, Steve Copses, Monique Giroux, Jon Greenberg, Sean Harlin, Tim Hevly, Jay Horwitz, Kerri Moore, Jim Moorehead, Lisa Ramsperger, Scott Reifert, Blake Rhodes, Rich Rice, Glen Serra, Kevin Shea, Chris Stathos, Jay Stenhouse, Bill Stetka, Bart Swain, Mike Swanson, Leigh Tobin, Jim Trdinich, Rick Vaughn, and Jim Young.

A very special thanks to John Olguin, Josh Rawitch, and Rachelle Smith of the Dodgers; Tim Mead and

Nancy Mazmanian of the Angels; Luis Garcia of the Padres; and Linda McNabb of the Miracle. You were all tremendous.

Thank you also to the hundreds of Major League players I interviewed; without you this book would only be a dream. Your graciousness with your time, energy and insights are greatly appreciated.

My sincere gratitude to Mike Veeck; without his help none of this would have happened.

Thank you to all my friends, teammates, and kids I coach for your valuable feedback on this project.

To my "All-Star" team: Michael Bernier, Andrea Reider and Colleen Wilson who went the extra innings to help with the production of this book.

To my "Home" team: my dad for signing me up for Little League, my mom for sewing all those patches on my first uniform, my sister, Marybeth, for her interest and support, my brothers, Tim, for always cheering me on and Trip, for making the first call to get the ball rolling on this book. Thanks also to my nephews Matt, Greg, Riley and Brayden for reminding me to play.

To my beautiful daughter and "Rookie of the Year", Janet Rose, for the purity and joy in her game. (And that one of her first words was "baseball!")

To my loving wife and "MVP", Christine, for her acceptance, encouragement and support of me and my vision. I am the luckiest man on the face of the earth!

Introduction

ongratulations for stepping up to the plate. You now have in your hands some of the BEST collective wisdom gathered from Major League Baseball's top players. After you read this book, you'll see how the game of baseball relates to life in a whole new way.

During the 2003 and part of 2004 baseball seasons, I interviewed over 300 players to find out how the game of baseball taught them about life—both on and off the field. They made a point of sharing their personal stories about the importance of teamwork, the meaning of success, how to overcome challenges and more. As a result, you've got an opportunity to learn from their experiences to become a better all-round person as well as improve as a player!

Like most kids, my first introduction to baseball was Little League, and my playing career went as far as college. I learned a lot of lessons from organized baseball as well as pick-up games my buddies and I played in back yards, open streets or neighborhood fields. Other than my parents and family, baseball has been one of the major influences in my life and still is today.

Baseball's allowed me to feel sad, mad, nervous, and silly with joy. It's taught me the meaning of teamwork, trust, discipline and perseverance. It's given me the opportunity to gain confidence, overcome failure and be humbled.

The experiences I've learned on the field have helped me get a better handle on the experiences I face off the field. Whenever I am challenged or need to understand something I ask myself, "How is what I'm going through now similar to something I've dealt with in baseball?" Once I figure out what the similarities are, I then ask myself, "How did I, or how would I, handle that situation in baseball?" Once I come up with an answer, I apply the 'baseball' concept to help me work through my current situation. I figure if I've experienced some sort of success or learned a lesson on the baseball field, it'll give me the confidence in life to face challenges at school, at home, with friends— pretty much anything.

Here's an example of what I mean. When I was in school, math was VERY hard. I remember a test I got back in which I didn't do very well. I was real mad because I missed questions I'd normally get right. Obviously, I wanted to do better. So I asked myself, "How is doing poorly on this math test similar to a situation in baseball?" ERRORS! Sometimes in games, I'd make an error on a play I'd normally make. The next day at practice, I'd work on fixing the error. I'd try to simplify things. For example I'd ask someone to roll ground balls that I could easily field with my bare hands. Once I felt confident, I'd challenge myself a little more. I'd put my glove on and have someone hit me some light grounders. As my confidence grew, I'd field a lot of ground balls that were similar to the error I made in the game. After repeated success, I was no longer concerned about the error and felt completely confident to move on.

What's the baseball-life similarity in this example? There could be many, but for me it's going back to the basics and simplifying things. With my math test, I went back to easier problems to solve (just like fielding rolled grounders bare handed). Once I got the hang of that, I moved on to more challenging math problems to solve (like fielding ground balls with my glove). That helped to build my confidence and work on the types of problems I missed on the test (or baseball game).

Paul Molitor, Hall of Famer (2003), said, "Look at each day as a new opportunity." You have a new chance on the next play, the next test, or the next day. Learn from the past to make yourself better.

This book is more than just advice from Major League players on how to play baseball. It's a way for you to look for, and make the most of, opportunities by matching "life" situations with "baseball" situations. That way you can have a better understanding and feel more confident in the things you do.

Lastly, whenever you feel you are up against a challenge, let this book be a source of inspiration. Allow it to help you take the proper actions and make the right choices, so you can reach out and help others just like these ball players have done for you.

Remember, these Major Leaguers were kids, just like you. They wanted to be heard, just like you. They had dreams, just like you. And they made their dreams come true, just like you can.

It's time to step up to the plate and play ball!

Editor's note: Players are listed in alphabetical order. Additionally, I recognize that English may not be the native language of some players. So in order to make the quotes more reader-friendly, slight modifications were made to keep the overall intention and meaning.

"Be your best and your best will see you through."
— BUCK O'NEIL

"You're given gifts. Our responsibility is to try to maximize those gifts."
— PAUL MOLITOR

CHAPTER 1

R-E-S-P-E-C-T
What Does It Mean?

"If you have to think about what's right or wrong, it's probably wrong."

—TREVOR HOFFMAN

Baseball has many long-standing traditions, most of which are unwritten and understood by the players. The tradition of respect is probably tops on the list.

The players gave a wide range of definitions or examples of respect: Respect for the game, the players and teammates, the uniform, the fans, even the people who work the game. The list goes on.

The word "respect" seems to be very prevalent today. People talk about not getting enough respect, needing respect, giving up too much respect.

What does respect look like? How do you know if you're getting respect or not? And what about things or objects, do they deserve the same kind of respect we give people?

In a ball game it's the little, sometimes unnoticed, things that can make a big difference that players have come to respect: A batter making a sacrifice bunt to move a runner into scoring position, a player coming early to hit in the batting cages, or a player giving a word of encouragement to a teammate.

Those same "little things," or signs of respect can make a difference off the field too: throwing a piece of paper in the garbage instead of on the ground, keeping walls free from graffiti or saying something nice about someone.

With all the different meanings of respect the players shared with me, their definitions fell into three main areas: respect in general, respect for people and respect for the game. You'll notice some overlap with their definitions or examples in different areas. Write down your definition of respect and see which player(s) match up best with it!

GENERAL

"Whenever someone does something wrong you teach them without yelling. Whenever someone does something good you don't yell at them. You say, 'Way to go! Nice job!' That is respect to me."

Bobby Abreu, *Aragua, Venezuela*

"Respect is something that has to be taught. There are a lot of different kinds of respect. Respect is treating people how you want to be treated and knowing right from wrong."

Brian Fuentes, *Merced, California*

"It's looking at people who you aspire to be like. Sometimes it's people who aren't exactly what you want to be, but you try to learn and understand why they are the way they are. You have to respect other players' talents. As soon as you don't respect something, whether it is a power tool or another hitter, you're going to get hurt."

Roy Halladay, *Denver, Colorado*

"Simply put, if you have to think about what's right or wrong, it's probably wrong. Bottom line, if you have to think about whether you need to spit on the sidewalk to be cool, you're not being respectful. If you're wearing your uniform in a way that is different, you're probably not giving the game respect. If you're doing something on the field that is pretty good and you show up another

TAKING STEPS

"I'd never try to embarrass somebody or yell bad (things) to him."

—AL KALINE

player by over celebrating, you're probably not giving that person respect. If those things go through your head, then it's probably not the thing to do."

Trevor Hoffman, *Bellflower, California.*

"I was brought up to respect everybody. I didn't want to do anything to disrespect my parents by getting in trouble.

(As a baseball player), you fear nobody, but you respect them. You don't say, 'I can't do this or I can't do that.' I'd never tear down a player or a pitcher I happen to have good luck or could do good things against. I knew he had a family to feed and he was doing the best he could.

I'd never try to embarrass somebody or yell bad (things) to him. Respect is a guy who does the very best he can day in and day out, whether it's in a factory or anything else. You do your job and give the people their due because they're trying to do the best they can and you respect them for that. So treat the game with the greatest of respect, as if it hasn't always been this good."

Al Kaline, *Baltimore, Maryland Hall of Fame, 1980*

"You know what's right and wrong. You know when you're doing something right or wrong. Being respectful is doing the right thing. That would be my simplest explanation."

Mark Kotsay, *Whittier, California*

"Respect is something you need to earn by how you carry yourself and what you are willing to invest in your responsibility. It's not something you can demand."

Tony La Russa, *Tampa, Florida*

"Respect comes from a lot of different things. It's doing your job as well as you can and correctly. It's being honest and giving your best effort. Having integrity is a big thing about respect. Doing what you say you're going to do."

Mark Loretta, *Santa Monica, California*

"You know your opponent is trying to do the same thing you are doing. They're trying to succeed. It's important your success does not mean any more than what it means. You scored a run, you hit a home run or you struck somebody out. That is all. You're not trying to make it more than it is. It's part of the game. You don't have to remind people they struck out or remind the whole place you hit a home run. Play the game right."

Mike Mussina, *Williamsport, Pennsylvania*

"Respect is anybody who handles himself with integrity and with dignity. In the most literal sense, treat someone how you would want to be treated."
Michael Young, *Covina, California*

PEOPLE

"No matter how good you are, you're no bigger than anyone else."
Carlos Beltran, *Manati, Puerto Rico*

"It's people appreciating you for who are, not so much what you do. I played with guys who have the utmost respect for their teammates. Those are the guys I want to hang around with."
Joe Girardi, *Peoria, Illinois*

"When you walk by somebody you look them in the eye and you say hello. You acknowledge that person. That is the easiest thing you can do. I learned this when I was 17 years old. I was the number one draft pick by the New York Yankees. They flew me from Fresno California to New York City to meet George Steinbrenner. When I met him I knew it was important to dress nice and make a good first impression. I wore a suit. I shook his hand firmly. As part of respect I looked him in the eye and said, 'Nice to meet you. Yes sir. No sir.' I had manners. He loved that. He wrote me a letter years later when he traded me to Baltimore. He told me he liked

TAKING STEPS

"Respect is knowledge and acknowledgment of the things people have done before us.

—BARRY LARKIN

me from the very first time I shook his hand. So that told me a lot about respect—shaking hands, looking people in the eye and acknowledging people."

Rex Hudler, *Tempe, Arizona*

"Respect is knowledge and acknowledgment of the things people have done before us. It's an appreciation of the history of our craft of baseball. To not be aware of those people, their accomplishments and their struggles, is a lack of respect."

Barry Larkin, *Cincinnati, Ohio*

"There are people who've come before you that have put in the time and given us opportunities. You have to appreciate that. They set the groundwork for all the good things we have today."

Mike Lowell, *San Juan, Puerto Rico*

"Respect, especially in my country, is really important. We use different language for older people, even if someone is one year older than me, out of respect."

Chan Ho Park, *Kongju, South Korea*

"It's showing your appreciation to (players with more experience). When they tell you something, you take it in. You might not respect a younger player who tells you something as much as you would a 15 year veteran. You're honored to have (guys like that) around."

Brad Penny, *Broken Arrow, Oklahoma*

"It's showing gratitude and appreciation for a particular person by a nice smile and a handshake. That's a sign of respect."

Reggie Sanders, *Florence, South Carolina*

"Respect is giving people their space and showing gratitude at the right situation. Being humble would be the best way to show respect. If you get too high on yourself and you turn your nose on someone, they won't respect you. If you keep a level head and stay the same person you think you should be, not only will you show respect to people, you'll also receive it."

Mike Timlin, *Midland, Texas*

"Henry Aaron respected people and the game by not letting it get to his head that he was any different than anyone else. We're all in this together. Some players are better than others. The bottom line is we're all human beings and we all deserve the same respect."

Robin Yount, *Danville, Illinois Hall of Fame, 1999*

GAME

"Respect is a discipline. It's being a professional. I am going to play as hard as I can and try to win."

Andruw Jones, *Willemstad, Curacao*

"You understand what guys had been through to get here and the reasons you're playing the game. Just like in daily life you treat people with respect because you want to be respected back. If you play the game with respect and respect the game, the game will treat you right."

Derek Lee, *Sacramento, California*

"I've worn the same helmet since 1998. Some players slam them, throw them or break them after they make an out or strike out. They go through five helmets a year. The thing about my helmet is I respect the situation. It's more of showing class and respect. That's how you gain respect. I learned to take care of my helmet in high school. I had a bad temper in high school and I used to throw my stuff. Then I watched

---

TAKING STEPS

"Respect is a discipline."

—ANDRUW JONES

---

big league players on TV. After they made an out, they just put their helmet down and put the batting gloves down. 'That's it,' I said. 'I'm never going to throw my helmet.' And I started making those adjustments."

Kevin Millar, *Los Angeles, California*

"Never think you're that much better than your opponent. The minute I start thinking, 'I'm a better pitcher than this guy is a hitter,' you're getting rocked. That's the way it is. The minute you get too cocky saying, 'I'm way better than this team, they can't hit me,' they will. Every day I'm learning something. I don't have it figured out."

Mark Mulder, *South Holland, Illinois*

"You have to be taught respect and you have to earn respect. I learned it all from my parents. One of the rules I had growing up was to play the game as hard as I could, respect the coaches and umpires. If I did those three things, I could play. If I didn't follow those rules, I wasn't allowed to play."

Curt Schilling, *Anchorage, Alaska*

"It's a privilege to put a uniform on and play the game at our level, even as a little leaguer. The game really does not ask anything of you. The baseball diamond is there for you to do what you want with it. If you want to play hard and work hard at it, you're going to be successful. If you're not and just think you're going to show up and be good, then the game is going to beat you. When you step on the field, you have to respect the game. That's not show boating or doing dances after you hit a home run or strike somebody out. Respect the game for what it is and treat it the same every day. Go out and play and see what happens."

J. T. Snow, *Long Beach, California*

"Respect is a guy who has a lot of work ethic. He's professional and is there for the team. You have to be responsible for what you're doing out there. A pitcher has a lot of responsibility for the team."

Ismael Valdez, *Ciudad Victoria, Tamaulipas, Mexico*

"It's being able to handle yourself and know yourself as a person when you're doing great things and getting the accolades. It's also being able to be the same professional person when you're down in the dumps and things aren't going your way. The toughest thing, mentally, for me to go through was arm surgery and missing a season—going to the field every day doing all my (rehab) and knowing when the game started, I was sitting on the bench and couldn't help. That made me stronger as a person. It made me love the game even more. I didn't respect the fact that I had a gift I was born with. I didn't take care of myself the way I should have and the game was taken away from me. I don't ever want to have that happen again. Therefore, I've got the respect for the game and myself to make sure I'm in mental and physical shape to play this game."

Kerry Wood, *Irving, Texas*

Step up to the challenge:

- How can you tell if a Major League ballplayer carries himself with high respect? What are his actions?
- Ask someone you respect what their definition is or if they have an example of what respect means. Then see if it matches up with a Major Leaguer!
- To stay on top of your game, list your strengths at being respectful. Where do you excel at being respectful? To improve upon your game, list where you can be better at being respectful.

Step out of the box to look for the signs

Try this for a week: As you go about your day, start to notice different signs of respect and disrespect. Why do you think people are respectful? Why do you think they are disrespectful?

CHAPTER **2**

Who Wants To Be On My Team?

"You need to look at what you can do to help your team win."

—ALBERT PUJOLS

Who makes up a team?

Obviously players or teammates do. But MAKING the team is only half of it. What's important is WHAT you bring to the team and HOW you bring it. And I don't mean just bringing your glove and your bat. I'm talking about what you contribute to the team. Your contribution as a teammate has an effect on how much success you'll have personally as well as how much success the team will have.

I look at a teammate as being more than just a player on a baseball team (or any sports team). Let's take it a step further. A teammate is anyone with whom you participate or spend time. For example: your family is a team; your friends are a team, your classmates and the people you hang out with at school are another team. So, whether you know it or not, you "play" on many different teams throughout your day. Remember, it's what you bring to these teams and how you bring it.

Here's another example: say you're invited to your best friend's birthday party. The party is the team and the guests are teammates. The "what" that you bring to the party is your friendship (to the others) and a gift to your best friend. The "how" is about caring and respect. Did you make an effort to show up on time to the party? Did you get something cool that your friend would like or could you've cared less about what you brought?

When I spoke with the Major Leaguers about teammates, I found there were basically two kinds— and ideal teammate, a player they would *want* on their team and an undesirable teammate, a player they would *not want* on their team.

The categories their comments fell into were: effort, support, and respect. As you read through the chapter, see if you can tell which kind of teammate the players are talking about. Their answers may surprise you!

EFFORT

"You have to be disciplined in this game. You're nothing without discipline. You could have great talent, but if you have a bad attitude, it's not a great role model for kids or anybody. So my guy plays with heart and has great discipline of the game."
Edgardo Alfonzo, *Santa Teresa, Venezuela*

"Somebody who goes out there plays hard and plays the right way. He gives everything he has to the club in order to win a baseball game."
Jeff Bagwell, *Boston, Massachusetts*

"Somebody who comes here for the paycheck. He hopes he doesn't play because he doesn't want to screw up. He's afraid to play or constantly says he can't play. And that's every day life too. Those people don't usually hang around too long."
Rod Beck, *Burbank, California*

"He puts the team first. He's responsible and conscientious. My mom and dad always told me to be responsible. It's like saying, 'Do the right thing'. The right thing isn't always the easy thing to do. It's not always the easiest path to take or the one that's going to make you the most popular. In the end, it's always the right way to go."
Craig Counsell, *South Bend, Indiana*

"Somebody who's just negative all the time, whining and never has anything good to say. They're selfish. You don't like to be around them because they can bring a whole team down."

Carl Crawford, *Houston, Texas*

"What sticks out most is work ethic. It tells me about his desire. Character and work ethic are the two things I look for in a baseball player. He'll go out on the field when there's nobody else around and be working on something by himself. They have a burning desire to play at higher level and it just sticks out."

Rick Dempsey, *Fayetteville, Tennessee*

"Players who point fingers at the ump, another teammate or have some sort of excuse why they didn't (perform). He's actually saying, 'Because of what this other person did, I'm unable to play to my ability.' I think it's a cop out. He should take responsibility and say, 'I messed up.'"

Morgan Ensberg, *Redondo Beach, California*

"A great teammate doesn't have to be a star on the team; it's the example he leads in the clubhouse and off the field. Some guys you look to as an example or to encourage you. If you get one guy that can do all those things, that's a wonderful teammate."

Joe Girardi, *Peoria, Illinois*

"It's selfish people who are just worried about themselves. They don't show up to play every day. They feel like they deserve some kind of special treatment. I don't pay them any attention. I try to stay as far away from them as possible."
Todd Helton, *Knoxville, Tennessee*

"Someone who is genuinely into the game. Whether he is playing nine innings or not playing at all, there's a way you can help the ball club. It's being supportive. Mark Langston (ML career, 1984-1999) always said, 'Be a fountain and not a drain.' Always find a way to build someone up instead of break them down."
Trevor Hoffman, *Bellflower, California*

"Anybody that works hard fits in on the team. You can be an outsider coming to a new team and if you work hard, you'll fit in no matter what job you're doing."
Tom Kelly, *Graceville, Minnesota*

TAKING STEPS

"A great teammate doesn't have to be a star on the team.
—JOE GIRARDI

"It's somebody you can count on and really depend on every night. They play the game the way it's suppose to be he played—hard. It's pretty much what anybody wants."

Jason Kendall, *San Diego, California*

"He leads by example. He doesn't have to tell somebody how do something. He's doing it himself and guys see him doing that. That's the best way to show somebody how to act on the field and off."

Joe Nathan, *Houston, Texas*

"My biggest thing is competitiveness; never giving up an atbat, diving after balls you think you can catch, never being afraid to take the ball as a pitcher. So many times you run into people that give in. When you can find a teammate that can give you 100 percent every day and be there for his teammates, that's big for me."

Troy Percival, *Fontana, California*

"A guy that hustles. A guy who's not afraid to show a little bit of emotion. Hard working is the number one thing and respectful."

A.J. Pierzynski, *Bridgehampton, New York*

"Someone you can count on. There's no guessing what you're going to get. Somebody who can be held accountable and you can trust what they're going to do, preparation-wise."

Tim Salmon, *Long Beach, California*

"Guys that are dogs. They don't work hard or play hard. Guys who aren't respectful. You can tell guys that aren't team players. They're all about themselves. There's nothing wrong with wanting to succeed for yourself, but it's a team and there's one goal and that's to win."

Chase Utley, *Pasadena, California*

"Someone who plays unselfishly and works hard. I'll take those things over someone just a little more talented."

Jason Veritek, *Rochester, Michigan*

"Somebody that hits a pop-up to the infield and doesn't run it out or hits a ground ball to the infield and doesn't run as fast as they can to first base is dogging it. You don't need any talent to put forth effort."

Matt Williams, *Bishop, California*

"When times are tough and they don't have it, they still believe they can get the job done. It's easy to smile when everything's going good, but when you're struggling, it shows your character. It's not so much getting it done, it's showing everyone, no matter what the situation, you still want the ball."

Dontrelle Willis, *Alameda, California*

SUPPORT

"Older guys who've been around have given me a lot of great advice. You have to take that in. I've talked to friends on other teams, that don't have those kind of leaders willing to give advice to the other guys."

Marcus Giles, *San Diego, California*

"Someone who seemed like they had it all figured out or they didn't want to try to get better. They're uncoachable."

Roy Halladay, *Denver, Colorado*

"You surround yourself with positive people you feel you can talk to and they pump you up to build confidence. Baseball is built on confidence. I want to be around a guy that's confident and positive. I just stay away from guys that are negative, full of excuses and don't care. In this game you have to care."

Torii Hunter, *Pine Bluff, Arkansas*

"Guys who aren't willing to share information, especially guys who are more experienced. One of the best things a veteran has to offer is what's inside his head. If a guy's been in the league for a long time there's

---

TAKING STEPS

"I want to be around a guy that's confident and positive."

—TORII HUNTER

a reason and he probably has a lot to offer a younger player. It's almost a shame not to."

Gary Matthews Jr., *San Francisco, California*

"A guy who's out there for himself, trying to do too much and not friendly. If I were the captain on the team, I'd bring him aside and try to talk to him. Maybe it's something off the field that's a problem. I'd try to address him first before I do to the whole team."

Joe Mauer, *St. Paul, Minnesota*

"I look at teammates as supporting each other or becoming competitive with each other to make each other better. We overcome those difficult times together. We help each other out and support each other, like a friend."

Hideo Nomo, *Osaka, Japan*

"It's a teammate to tell me he sees something I'm doing different. I had a shortstop tell me during a game my curveball wasn't coming out of my hand properly. So I'll try to work on it during the game."

Roy Oswalt, *Kosciusko, Mississippi*

"It's a game that demands enthusiasm and support. A pat on the back goes a long way whether you're somebody's teammate or coach. When somebody was there to pump me up and encourage me, it gave me the incentive to do better. That makes a difference in a lot of guys' days or a lot of guys' seasons. That's very, very important."

Lance Parrish, *Clairton, Pennsylvania*

"Somebody that's going to be supporting you all the time no matter if you're doing good or bad. There's a lot of jealousy in this game. Guys will be struggling and sometimes won't have anything to do with you if you're not going good. That's the quality of a terrible teammate. You want somebody who has a good attitude. Someone who's humble and takes everything in stride."

Andy Pettitte, *Baton Rouge, Louisiana*

"A ball player who can adjust to every situation, because you are in a room with different personalities and people with different backgrounds. You have to know how to adjust to any given (situation)."

Reggie Sanders, *Florence, South Carolina*

"He puts the team before himself. I'm not a big fan of sarcastic people or negative people. I like being around guys who are always positive. Guys who can take the time to pat a teammate on the back. It's somebody going out of his way to lift somebody else even when they are struggling."

Gregg Zaun, *Glendale, California.*

RESPECT

"He's a guy who is selfish. He's making jokes if we lost and acts like he doesn't care. You don't want those guys to be a part of your team because they're like a bad fruit. One bad fruit is going to destroy the rest of the fruit."
Bobby Abreu, *Aragua, Venezuela*

"A guy that's a team player is not afraid to share secrets. Every time we come to the ballpark he wants to go over the pitcher we're facing. He wants to tell me what he does at the plate against the pitcher. A (team player) cares about the team, cares about how each individual is doing."
Frank Catalanotto, *Smithtown, New York*

"I learn from everybody, both good and bad qualities. You learn from that and say, 'I'm not going to do that. That's not me.' The qualities of a good person stays focused and knows what he's doing. He knows what life's all about. I just stay away from (the bad teammate)."
Eddie Guardado, *Stockton, California*

TAKING STEPS

"I learn from everybody, both good and bad qualities."

—EDDIE GUARDADO

"If you're putting down other players for making mistakes, I don't like that. When I was younger, I used to get mad and say, 'Man, he's messing up.' Then I'd step back and say, 'I don't make every single play. He's trying to do the best he can to make every play.' It's not your job to put that guy down because he's not doing it how you could do it or how you think he should be doing it. When you make sure everything is right with you, and you're doing everything you can to help your team win, that's the guy I want to be with."

Jacque Jones, *San Diego, California*

"He'd be a loyal, trustworthy person dedicated to the job while they're here and dedicated to family when they're not. A big part of a person is how they handle themselves on and off the field."

Mark Kotsay, *Whittier, California*

"My ideal teammate is somebody that works hard to help the team. He respects the space of his teammates inside the clubhouse, on the plane, on the bus—the working environment. Somebody that takes pride in his performance both on and off the field."

Greg Maddux, *San Angelo, Texas*

"Players who are constantly looking out for their own well-being are the ones not trusted. The guys you're with consistently, six months of the season, really see what you are made of. They see what your motivation is and what kind of person you truly are."

Mike Matheny, *Columbus, Ohio*

"I like a clean living guy. My whole career, my one purpose, my motivating force was to always make my parents proud. If I did that then I knew I was never going to get in trouble. That's how I operated. I worked hard to be a success in this game so my parents would be proud."

Jack McKeon, *South Amboy, New Jersey*

"He's someone that has a tendency to jump all over his teammates. Someone who doesn't take accountability for his mistakes and always has excuses. Someone that's disrespectful to other players, other teams or umpires."

Paul Molitor, *St. Paul, Minnesota.*
Hall of Fame, 2003

"You win as a team and you lose as a team. I am around my teammates for about eight months out of the year. Whether you like them or dislike them, you have to find a way to get along. You learn about yourself and you learn about other people."

Jamie Moyer, *Sellersville,*
Pennsylvania

"Somebody that doesn't respect the game. I've played with some players that may have been good players, but

TAKING STEPS

"It's not your job to put that guy down because he's not doing it how you think he should be doing it."

—JACQUE JONES

not good teammates. It's guys who don't feel like playing that day and go through the motions. You really figure out who the quality guys are on your team. You can't rely on them to give you a hundred percent."

Phil Nevin, *Fullerton, California*

"Somebody who's a leader of the team can have a huge impact on the team. He might be the best player, but it doesn't matter because he's making other players on the team feel bad by bringing them down when they make a bad play."

John Olerud, *Seattle, Washington*

"I played with one of the best pitchers I ever caught in my life. He's out of baseball right now because of the way he acted. Nobody liked him because he was always talking bad about everybody."

Eddie Perez, *Ciudad Ojeda, Venezuela*

"You always want to have good teammates to motivate yourself and to get yourself better. If you want to be a winner, you need to look at what you can do to help your team win. That's what it's all about, helping each other out like a brother."

Albert Pujols, *Santo Domingo, Dominican Republic*

"There are people that aren't the character people you want to be hanging out with, but you don't treat those people poorly. You always treat people the way you want to be treated. And you take the high road. If that's not good enough then you walk away."

Alex Rodriguez, *New York, New York*

"The ideal teammate is accountable. They say, 'Hey, I made an error today and it cost us the game. I take full responsibility for that. I make no excuses for my play or who I am.'"

Scott Rolen, *Evansville, Indiana*

"The most important thing is that my teammates respect each other like a family."

Alfonso Soriano, *San Pedro de Macoris, Dominican Republic*

"A guy who's jealous and wishes other guys on the team aren't doing well just to make himself shine. A guy that isn't really sure of who he is and looks for his own security in other people's failure."

Barry Zito, *Las Vegas, Nevada*

Step up to the challenge:

- If you were making up a "team," what qualities would you want in a teammate? How similar are they to the players you read about in this chapter?
- Using the idea of a birthday party to figure out what a teammate brings, how well do you get along with or receive your teammates?
- What can you learn and appreciate about your opponents—the "players" on other "teams" (or people with whom you don't hang out)?

Step out of the box to look for the signs

Try this for a week: As you go about your day, start to notice how people on other "teams" act. What are the reasons you MIGHT want to be on their team? What are the reasons you wouldn't want to be on their team?

CHAPTER 3

I Don't Think I Smell, But They Tell Me I Stink!

"I don't let anything pass from my head into my heart."

—MIGUEL TEJADA

"**B**ooooo! You stink! You're a bum! Hey catcher, you can't throw anyone out. You probably couldn't throw out the garbage! You're the worst pitcher I've ever seen! You've got no business wearing that uniform. You can't hit... You're terrible!" And on and on it goes.

It happens from game to game, stadium to stadium, and city to city. When you go to a game and you hear the fans booing or calling players names, do you ever stop to wonder what the player is thinking? Sure the players are tough, but do you think it hurts their feelings? How do they deal with all that heckling?

Baseball can be difficult to play even without fans and players screaming and yelling at you. We've all been yelled at, called names and teased for a variety of reasons—some more than others. And it can be challenging not to get wrapped up in what people are saying and yelling at you.

Some players believe if they hear something enough times, there must be some truth to it; so then they start to believe it. The key is to recognize the difference between someone's opinion about you as a player, and the truth. Catcher Greg Zaun said, "I don't reflect upon myself as a poor player, just a player that had a poor performance." (More about that in chapter 4).

So, if we know teasing is going to happen and people are going to yell and scream at us and call us names, what can we do about it? How can we make the best of the situation? What do the pros do to stay positive in a game that is built on failure and can be negative? That's what this chapter is about—Big Leaguers really letting you know what they think about hecklers, but more importantly, how they handle being teased and called names.

"Don't pay any attention to it. That's easy to say. If you prioritize the people you care about it's not going matter what they think. If you care about what your coach, your teammates and your family think, it keeps it pretty simple."
David Bell, *Cincinnati, Ohio*

"I just remain focused on what I'm trying to do. Maybe in my younger days I might react to it. Now, it means nothing. How did I get to that point? I realize what I'm trying to do. I'm trying to help the team by doing my job successfully. And the only way I can do my job is to be 100 percent focused on it. If I'm thinking about this guy's a jerk because he's yelling at me or saying I stink, that's a distraction. I just learned what I needed to focus on to do my job successfully."
Jeremy Burnitz, *Westminster, California*

"There are times when people get on you you're thinking, 'That's mean. Why would you say that to somebody just because we are baseball players?' We're still human beings. We don't go to somebody's office and sit over them and say, 'You're not typing right! That was a terrible phone call you just made! You stink. You're a bum!' That gets old after awhile. You treat people the way you want to be treated.

For example: A guy got on me the other night, he's yelling, 'Cut your hair! Cut your hair!' every time I came up to bat. I think he had a few drinks. I wanted to be mean back, but instead of being mean back, I brought him a glass of water. I said, 'Here you go.

You might want to have this so you feel better tomorrow morning.' He kind of lightened up and said, 'Thanks a lot for the water!' When people get on me, I kill them with kindness. I'm not going to bury you. I'm going to show you that I'm a nice guy and what you're saying to me is not affecting me.

When people yell at you, they want you to yell back. That's not the way to go. If you snap and play his game, now you're yelling at him and he's yelling you, what does that accomplish? What does it accomplish when two people fight? It accomplishes nothing. If you can talk about it and get things out, that's a better way to go."

Sean Casey, *Willingboro, New Jersey*

"Nobody likes to be called names. We are no different than a Little Leaguer. I don't really think it's your friends calling you names. If people I really respect are calling me names, then you take that to heart a little more. People who don't know me, it kind of rolls off my back."

Craig Counsell, *South Bend, Indiana*

TAKING STEPS

"Nobody likes to be called names. We're no different than a Little Leaguer."

—CRAIG COUNSELL

"You have to realize you belong out there. People are only trying to bring you down to better themselves. If you show them it doesn't bother you and play through that, eventually they'll stop."

Michael Cuddyer, *Norfolk, Virginia*

"People will call you names out of the blue ever since you were in Little League. The only way you get used to that is to continue to go through it. It's an ugly side of the game, but you know what? It's there. Either let it bother you, or you can let it make you stronger. Over time, you just develop almost a numbness to it. You just have to accept that it's not personal and you can't take it with emotion."

Darin Erstad, *Jamestown, North Dakota*

"You try to block everything out. When I was young I always got teased and all that stuff. People who talk bad are always jealous of you anyway. It's just a waste of time and energy to worry about it. It's negative. You got to think positive and not worry about those guys. I don't."

Eric Gagne, *Montreal, Petit-Quebec, Canada*

TAKING STEPS

"You got to think positive and not worry about those guys. I don't."

—ERIC GAGNE

"I just have fun with it. I just say, 'You're right.' Fans want guys to bark back at them or curse back at them. Then they're going to rag you even more. But if you just smile and say, 'You're right,' usually they don't have much left to say."

Mark Grace, *Winston-Salem, North Carolina*

"I just let them have their fun. If you yell back or cuss back at them, that just makes you look bad for the (people) around that see that."

Danny Graves, *Saigon, South Vietnam*

"You have to realize, people are going to take you out of your game by personal attacks, calling you names and stuff like that. Part of being successful is learning how to tune all that stuff out and staying focused on what's happening between the lines. Concentrate on the pitcher or what you're going to do if the ball is hit to you."

Chipper Jones, *DeLand, Florida*

"I take it in stride. I was a short chubby kid when I was little, so I got a lot of razzing and stuff like that. I still get razzed because I am short. I just laugh right back at them or I say something right back at them. You have to take it in stride. You can't take it serious. Have fun with it. You take it serious, it starts getting in your head. It doesn't bother me."

Paul Lo Duca, *Brooklyn, New York*

TAKING STEPS

*"I use it as a tool.
(It) tells me I'm not focusing ...
on what I need to do."*

—JAMIE MOYER

"When those things happen and people call me names, I use it as a tool. Focus and concentration are very important to me. If I'm pitching and I hear somebody in the stands, or even in the upper deck, saying, 'Moyer you stink!' or 'Throw strikes,' I try not to let it draw my attention away. I say, 'This tells me I'm not focusing. I need to step off the rubber and try to refocus on what I need to do.'"

Jamie Moyer, *Sellersville, Pennsylvania*

"You learn to tune it out. I feel I've earned my spot. So for anybody else to say anything, they're not the ones who gave me the chance to play. At first it does affect you. You're thinking, 'Why is this person on me so much?' At the same time you just kind of tune it out and be confident knowing that you're good enough. If you let the (negative) affect you, then you are not preparing yourself to do your job."

Russ Ortiz, *Encino, California*

"It's tough. It's something you have to be able to block out. I continually make those mental efforts to stay in the game. 'What's the situation? What am I going to do when the ball is hit to me?' That will help me get out of whatever it is they're saying. You don't have to turn and acknowledge them because that tends to spurn on more of it. Sometimes you can laugh with them. Don't take yourself too seriously."

Tim Salmon, *Long Beach, California*

"Just take it. Sit there and listen to them. Anything that can take you off what you're doing, the other person's been successful. I am a big person to let character stand the test of time."

John Smoltz, *Detroit, Michigan*

"If somebody is attacking me as a person, I close my eyes immediately and say, 'God, give me strength to get through this and not act like he's acting.' I think name calling and picking on kids is usually brought on by peer pressure. (It's) guys who want to be cool in front of other friends or try to chop off someone's head to make them look taller. But a real cool kid encourages his teammates to be better, makes his teammates feel good about themselves. That's what is necessary to have a winning team."

Mike Sweeney, *Orange, California*

"When I'm in the game I don't let anything pass from my head into my heart."

Miguel Tejada, *Bani, Dominican Republic*

"It used to really bother me. I'm human just like the next person. Now I try to take what they say and put them in the batter's box and use whatever bad energy they give me to my advantage."

Mike Timlin, *Midland, Texas*

"(The fans) can say anything they want. If you're going to believe that, you're going to have serious problems, because they're going to keep going and going. They try to get you mad. If you get mad you're doing them a favor. But if you don't care, they'll try to pick on another player."

Fernando Valenzuela, *Navojoa, Sonora, Mexico*

"You have to force yourself to ignore it. I've learned, as I got older, a lot of people base their self-worth on what other people think about you. You have to be happy with yourself. You have to be confident in yourself. A lot of that stems from the way you were brought up, from your parents and your friends. A lot

TAKING STEPS

"My self-worth is based on the type of person I am, not what I do on the field."

—TIM WAKEFIELD

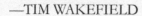

of people place everybody's self-worth on how much money they make or how successful they are in their jobs. My self-worth is based on the type of person I am, not what I do on the field."

Tim Wakefield, *Melbourne, Florida*

"Focus on your task. You have to realize people want to be where you are. You have to take it like that."

Brandon Webb, *Ashland, Kentucky*

"I rise above it. I realized if people are calling me names, it's either in fun, which most times it is here, so it's funny. But if there's some type of malicious intent, I just rise above it. I let it bead off me like water. I realize the people doing the name-calling are the ones truly hurting and struggling inside."

Barry Zito, *Las Vegas, Nevada*

Step up to the challenge:

- Which Big Leaguer's advice about dealing with hecklers did you like best?
- In your opinion, what's the point in calling someone a hurtful name?
- What are some positive things you can say to yourself when someone is putting you down?

Step out of the box to look for the signs

Try this for a week: As you go about your day, start to notice how you react when people insult you or say things that don't sit right with you. What's the feeling that comes up when you hear those words? What is a positive way for you to react to those words?

CHAPTER 4

Slaying The "Error Monster" And The "Slump Slug"!

"I don't reflect upon myself as a poor player, just a player that had a poor performance."

—GREGG ZAUN

They can show up in a game and sometimes last a week, a month, or half the season! Some are obvious. Some are subtle. But they never feel good when they happen, especially when you're involved—

ERRORS and SLUMPS!! They're like monsters in a horror movie, how do you survive?

On and off the field, we make errors, mistakes, even go through slumps in all areas of our lives. In school, taking a test is like playing in a baseball game. Both the school test and baseball game are "testing" you to see how good you are—that day. We all want to do well and sometimes when we don't, we can get down on ourselves and it can linger. Nobody is perfect.

Believe it or not, many of the players I spoke with feel the same way you do when things aren't going well. It doesn't make it any easier when it happens in front of a lot of people who are counting on you or are there to watch you play. The feeling can get worse when nothing seems to go your way and errors, bad games or bad days start piling up one after another.

So how do you deal with this "Error Monster" or "Slump Slug" when it rears its ugly head? When I spoke with the ball players, the four main areas that came up about dealing with errors are what I subtitled: acceptance, adjustments, control emotions, and staying positive.

Working on those four areas will help you build confidence for those games and tests.

ACCEPTANCE

"I don't think any one play loses a game. I think it contributes. If you have that perspective, 'I was a part of the reason we lost. I was not the only reason, but I was a part of the reason,' and not take it so personal, you can survive in this game. If you're prepared and you fail, you can keep your head high. But if you don't prepare and fail, then you are shortchanging your teammates. You're not respecting everyone else who puts on that uniform."

Larry Bowa, *Sacramento, California*

"It's just like making a wrong turn in a car, you just turn back around and keep going. If I make a mistake I just try to do the best I can and make the next play. It's pretty simple, you are expected to do the majority of things right. If you mess up one time it doesn't mean the whole day is a loss."

Jim Edmonds, *Fullerton, California*

"That's tough. I admit it. Last night I had a ball hit off my head. That's pretty embarrassing. You just got to

TAKING STEPS

"The most important thing is to simplify things."

—ROY HALLADAY

43

tell yourself it's over with. The worst thing you can do is be thinking about your at-bat in the field after you strike out and have a guy hit a ball over your head. If you have the mind-set of putting the team ahead of yourself and do your job, you'll be okay."

Jay Gibbons, *Rochester, Mississippi*

"Forget about it. You're going to do more good for your team than bad. Believe you're going to make the next play. Just concentrate on the next one. When the ball's hit to you, then you make that play. If you make an error move on. You may work on it the next day, but go out there and have some fun."

Ken Griffey Jr., *Donora, Pennsylvania*

"The most important thing is to simplify things down to making one pitch or just seeing the ball and hitting the ball. That's it. Sometimes if you give up a couple of runs, it's hard to relax and get back to that point. It's important for me to remember that no matter how much I want to, I can't change anything that has already happened. I can't control the future, I can't control the past. Really, the only thing I can control is what I'm doing at that very second. And that is my focus. I'm going to try and control this next pitch."

Roy Halladay, *Denver, Colorado*

"Baseball is a game of failure. You have to look at all that. If you don't accept failure, you can't succeed in the game. As I got older and more mature, I started to understand (to hit successfully) three out of ten times you're a hero. Three out of ten times in your grades is a flat out 'F.' I learned if I strikeout three times in a row that day, I wash it out. It's hard to do sometimes, but you've just got to wash it out and come back the next day. By 'wash it out,' I just try to clear it out of my head. I might go home and read my Bible, or play Play Station, go bowling or go to the movies, anything to take my mind off it. Remember, this is my career!"

Torii Hunter, *Pine Bluff, Arkansas*

"It bothers you that you made a mistake. What makes me bounce back is, just like in any other workplace, there are other people counting on you. You have to put your feelings aside, not be selfish and get the job done because people are counting on you."

Paul Konerko, *Providence, Rhode Island*

"The people I'm playing against are competing just as hard as I am to get a hit, get on base or score a run, whatever the case. Everybody playing this game has to realize that. Somebody's going to succeed and somebody's going to fail. Whether you succeed or not, you have to throw the next pitch or take that next atbat and keep going. If you keep going, eventually it comes around and you get your piece of success too. There is a lot to learn from failing seven times out of ten and still being a success. Errors are part of the game. You have to experience and learn for yourself."

Mike Mussina, *Williamsport, Pennsylvania*

TAKING STEPS

*"Nobody's perfect.
Just learn from your mistakes."*

—IVAN RODRIGUEZ

"You ask yourself what you could have done differently. If you can learn from it and move on, then the error is no longer a failure. You turn it into a positive. Everything should be a learning experience whether in baseball or in life. You should always ask yourself, 'Is there something I could've done different?' If not, then let it go."

Josh Phelps, *Anchorage, Alaska*

"Nobody's perfect. If you're perfect you should play another level and there's not another level above the Major Leagues. Just learn from your mistakes."

Ivan Rodriguez, *Manati, Puerto Rico*

"There is more than one aspect of the game, whether it be throwing a guy out, making a great catch or making a slide to break up a double play to keep the inning alive. When one thing is not going well, you can contribute another way. To walk back to the dugout because a guy struck you out is part of life. You better get used to it."

Larry Walker, *Maple Ridge, British Columbia, Canada*

"I learned in 'Double A' ball in Midland, Texas, the most important thing is how to deal with failure and not letting it affect me into the next pitch, next batter or the next game. Every start I'd do worse and I'd take it into the next start. I was mentally beating myself up. Finally I just said, 'You know what, let's go back out and have fun. Do what I've always loved doing and just have fun playing the game. If I give up a home run, if I have a bad game, I can't go back and change it so there's no sense in getting mad.' Now I've become really good at being able to discard any negative thoughts on the mound. If I make a bad pitch or give up a home run, I don't mentally beat myself up any more because I can't change it. That's helped me move forward. Being able to deal with the failures is one of the most important parts of being successful."

Jarrod Washburn, *LaCrosse, Wisconsin*

TAKING STEPS

*"I write things down ...
So when I get into a rut, I can review it."*
—MATT CLEMENT

ADJUSTMENTS

"I started to write things down when I'm pitching good and what works. So when I get into a rut I can review what I've written down over the years. Maybe one thing will let me know what I'm not doing well. My goal is to become as consistent as I can. What helps me is to write it down. Pitching coach Larry Rothschild helped me with that."

Matt Clement, *McCandless Township, Pennsylvania*

"Baseball is a game of concentration and repetition. You always move forward. What's the next play? The next moment is always what's important. Once a moment is over, you have to go to the next moment. That's how the game works. Your concentration level has to be kept high for the whole game. That's how I forget about errors. For me to succeed, I have to be 100 percent focused on what's going to happen, not what has happened. I always look forward."

Craig Counsell, *South Bend, Indiana*

"I've always been told to step off a mound, walk around and take a couple of deep breaths and forget about it. A good baseball player has a good short-term memory. They can put stuff behind them and learn from it in the long run."

Josh Fogg, *Lynn, Massachusetts*

"I visualize every pitch (the type of pitch) and the location I want before I throw it. If you train your mind to be positive and visualize that positive pitch, it's amazing how many times the results turn out the way you want. It's just a split-second thing you can do. It reinforces the positive."

Chad Fox, *Houston, Texas*

"I trained myself from a kid to challenge myself (about making) errors. I learned that I'm going to benefit from it. I learned to keep building that foundation. If you worry about making errors, you're going to make errors, you never benefit from it. You learn from the challenge. When you make an error you learn how to work and correct those things. That's the way you become successful. Any time you go on the field, you should come off the field learning something good or bad."

Willie Horton, *Arno, Virginia*

"You step back, take a deep breath and you go back to locating your pitches. Gil Patterson and Mark Connor, pitching coaches, told me the most important pitch is

TAKING STEPS

"Even if you drop a ball,
you still got to make a play."

—DAVE ROBERTS

your next pitch. You got to go out there and battle. You know someone is good if they can get through that."

Brad Penny, *Broken Arrow, Oklahoma*

"It's tough. Coach Adams (from) UCLA always told me that baseball is a game of quick recovery. Even if you drop a ball, you still got to make a play and try to throw the guy out—as opposed to getting upset you missed the ball and don't finish the play. The people that can recover quicker and limit their mistakes are also the ones that are the best."

Dave Roberts, *Okinawa, Japan*

"If I give up a home run, walk a batter or give up a base hit, I try to make an adjustment. I figure out what I can do to make the pitch better. I take every pitch like a photo. I see a picture in my mind before I throw and say, 'I want this pitch on the outside corner to a right-handed hitter.' I have some pitch in my mind I like and I just try to do the same thing."

Francisco Rodriguez, *Caracas, Venezuela*

"I worry about what I can control on the field and that's it. After the ball leaves my hand I can't control it. Guys make errors. Guys hit home runs. All I can control is being ready, staying focused and delivering the pitch."

C.C. Sabathia, *Vallejo, California*

"I take a nice deep breath, clear my mind and think about whatever situation is coming up. I'll repeat something in my head to not allow anything else in.

TAKING STEPS

"If you stay focused on what you're trying to do, it is a lot easier to forget what has just happened."

—ROBIN YOUNT

If I'm going to make a pitch, I'll just say, 'Glove, glove, glove' to myself to (focus) on the catcher's glove rather than think about what the coaches are thinking or anything going on in the stands. It helps me keep focused. To keep a little bit of a routine keeps me more in a comfort zone."

Steve Sparks, *Tulsa, Oklahoma*

"If I ever made an error my confidence really did go down. I'd get through that game the best I could and reflect on good games and positive things. You got to work on yourself. Nobody else can do it for you. The next day, I'd come out and take 25-40 groundballs bare-handed. When you field the ball without the glove, it makes you do everything right."

Maury Wills, *Washington, DC*

"If you stay focused on what you're trying to do, it is a lot easier to forget what has just happened. If you're thinking about the last one, then you're not focused on what you're about to do."

Robin Yount, *Danville, Illinois Hall of Fame, 1999.*

CONTROL EMOTIONS

"That's one thing about baseball that relates well to life, you're going to make errors and strike out. Everybody deals with it their own way. Some guys get really frustrated and blow up and that's the end of it. Some guys kind of hide their emotions, but it stays with them longer. The main point is, you've got to find some way mentally to block it out and be ready for the next play."

Lance Berkman, *Waco, Texas*

"You can't just throw your glove down and quit. The next play is always a new play. You can be upset with yourself, but you just have to find a way to channel it in a positive manner, rather than let it linger and cause you to lose focus on the game."

Milton Bradley, *Harbor City, California*

"I say to myself, 'There's nothing I can do about it now, it's over with.' The negativity from that error is only going to make things worse. I might make another error because now I'm not focused on what I need to focus on. Sometimes I'll smooth the dirt out or take my glove off for a second, take a deep breath and get back in the moment of what I'm trying to do. They say give yourself (a few) seconds of getting angry and then you got to move on."

Sean Casey, *Willingboro, New Jersey*

"I think a lot of my teammates look to me for leadership. I try not to show if I'm not hitting well, because I know those guys are looking at me to see how I react to things. I always try to stay at the same level. When you're hitting well, everything is going great. When you're not doing so well, that's the real test to see what kind of person you really are."

Luis Gonzalez, *Tampa, Florida*

"I do a lot of mental training. Before the game I always look at one point, like a flag or some advertising signs. When I see the flag, I remind myself, 'This is just baseball. Don't be too serious. Okay, back to baseball. Now I can pitch.' Also, I use deep breaths and that helps even if I don't give up any (runs). I use it as a routine. I walk off the mound, look at the flag, take a few deep breaths and then come back to the mound. A lot of guys do that."

Shigetoshi Hasegawa, *Kobe, Japan*

"There is a little routine a lot of big leaguers go through in between pitches. You see a little clump of dirt to smooth over that means, 'Okay, I'm starting over, clean the slate,' like you would a chalkboard. Erase it. When I find myself getting really tense and feeling the pressure of the game, I just take a deep breath. It helps me relax and slow everything down. When the nerves start going, the game starts speeding up. The guy who the game comes easy thinks, it's slow. But the guy who is struggling thinks the guy pitching is throwing a hundred miles an hour."

Joe Lawrence, *Lake Charles, Louisiana*

"It's just a matter of going through the process. When you're struggling you want to be around guys you respect and will keep you positive. I take a couple of deep breaths, nice and slow to slow my heartbeat down so I can clear my mind and focus. I do the same in the on-deck circle and even when I'm catching. That's something I've done over the years. I've taken yoga in the past to help me get to that state of mind when you're going well."

Mike Lieberthal, *Glendale, California*

"The process is very simple. You never throw a pitch while you are angry about the last pitch. The process is to recognize when you're no longer upset about the last pitch you've thrown. (You can) kick the grass, throw the rosin bag or give yourself a pep talk. Each day is

TAKING STEPS

"It's very important not to have the last pitch on my mind as I'm throwing my next pitch."

—GREG MADDUX

different. It's very important not to have the last pitch on my mind as I'm throwing my next pitch."

Greg Maddux, *San Angelo, Texas*

"Being a catcher is one of the tougher positions, because you're definitely going to be involved in the next play. I've always used deep breaths, taking my mask off to refocus. When my mask is on I'm 100 percent focused on what I'm doing. Positive thoughts are absolutely strengthening. You have to go to what you did well and not dwell on what you did wrong. I have a focal point at each stadium. When stuff goes wrong, it reminds me, 'I am good at this. I am good at what I do.' It pumps you back up."

Brad Moeller, *Upland, California*

"When you're in a slump, you got to come up with some short-term goals to help get you back on track. Your mind has a way of putting limitations on your goals. It's true in the classroom or at home. Nobody knows their

TAKING STEPS

"When you're in a slump, you got to come up with some short-term goals."

—PAUL MOLITOR

ceiling. There are going to be challenges and obstacles. That's how we develop the ability to persevere. When you persevere you're going to develop your character. That's how we become better people and better teammates. If you're not able to handle that and grow and learn from those things, it's going to be a tough road for you. Look at each at-bat as a new opportunity to get something going in the right direction."

Paul Molitor, *St. Paul, Minnesota Hall of Fame, 2003*

"You know what you did when you made the error. Turn around and take your hat off and get your mind right and know what you need to do differently. 'Okay, now the ball was hit here, make sure I stay down.' Just exaggerate things like you would if you were in practice. It gives you that confidence you'll catch the next ball hit to you. If you get scared because the fans start booing and they get on you, just take your time."

Jimmy Rollins, *Oakland, California*

"When you make an error or strike out, you feel like you're the only person in the ballpark being singled out. You think everybody is looking at you and talking about you. I've been guilty of this for a number of years. All this negative stuff just hits you. The truth is if you knew how little they actually thought about you, the way you think they do, you wouldn't worry so much about it."

Todd Walker, *Bakersfield, California*

"You have to deny the senses—what you see and know to be true. You have to go more with an inner feeling, an inner conviction, of how good you are or how good you can be. If you feel that in your heart enough, it'll play out. It's knowing who you are inside and it takes a diligent work, mentally, to do that."

Barry Zito, *Las Vegas, Nevada*

STAYING POSITIVE

"I just don't use the word 'slump.' A lot of guys say, 'What's a slump? I've never been in one. I don't know what a slump is.' That's where you have to forget about the past and say, 'I'm 0 for 0. I haven't played yet today.' You have to make everything positive."

Hank Blalock, *San Diego, California*

"What can I do to get us out of the situation we are in? What am I going to do when the ball is hit to me? If you focus on the negative, it's going to affect you for the next play. A lot of times I'm seeing how the pitchers are pitching and I'm riding the wave with them. They get into a tight situation and I'll find myself stressing out with them. It just clicked one day, 'Why am I worried about this? We're already in this situation, how are we going to get out of it?' You focus on the next play and it helps take your mind off what you just did."

Steve Finley, *Paducah, New York*

"You have to be able to check your emotions on the side. I've struggled with that. The other day, I gave up the game-winning run. I was real disappointed. I only had to get one out. (I wanted to) give my team a chance to come back. Unfortunately we didn't come back. I have to not worry about my feeling of letting the team down, 'We're going to lose because of me.' I needed to start thinking how can I help the team."

Brian Fuentes, *Merced, California*

"Every time I'm on the mound, I try to think about positive stuff. I think, 'What did I feel when I struck out Ken Griffey Jr., Mark McGwire, Sammy Sosa, the big guys I used to look up to?' That's a positive picture in my head. Anytime anything goes bad, I go back where it's all positive. You try to slow down everything and picture a positive—a strike out, a ground ball, whatever you need. That's what I try to do every time, every pitch."

Eric Gagne, *Montreal, Petit-Quebec, Canada*

"I just battle, do my drills and keep working. Eventually you come out of it. But in some ways you got to enjoy the struggles as much as you enjoy the good times. You tend to become a better player after the slump and after the struggles."

Shawn Green, *Des Plaines, Illinois*

"As a coach, the first thing I tell the guys is, 'Don't feel bad because you made an error. I'm not going to make an error because I'm not playing. The only people not

making errors are the ones not on the field.' Don't be afraid to make another one. Just go and play your game and hopefully you can help the team in a different way."
Ozzie Guillen, *Ocumare Del Tuy, Venezuela*

"Play with a positive outlook—what you're going to do as opposed to the negative of what you don't want to happen. If you are thinking about not making an error, more than likely you're going to make one."
Barry Larkin, *Cincinnati, Ohio.*

"After I get angry about what I've done, the first thing I say is, 'More opportunities like that are going to come.' So every time I make a mistake, rather than have a negative thought, I just learn from that."
Javy Lopez, *Ponce, Puerto Rico*

"The toughest part of the game is to learn how to deal with adversity. Simple, positive things you can tell yourself are very, very important. Just change the negative thought for a positive one. Then slowly you can

TAKING STEPS

Whatever you are thinking will help you relax or make you tense."
—EDGAR MARTINEZ

learn and be aware when that happens. When it does, you can talk to yourself in a positive way. You're ready for the next ground ball or the next at-bat. Whatever you are thinking will help you relax or make you tense."

Edgar Martinez, *New York, New York*

"It's tough to focus sometimes and some guys don't know what to focus on. You try to figure that out. It comes with a lot of trial and error. I try to focus on the very next pitch I'm going to make. Before I get on the rubber, I try to picture that pitch in my mind. And then when I get on the rubber, I just forget about it and throw the pitch. That seems to help me out a lot."

Kevin Milwood, *Gastonia, North Carolina*

"That is a learned environment. You have to go out there and get beat so many times before you learn there's going to be a tomorrow. There's going to be a next pitch. You have to experience failure before you know how to handle failure."

Troy Percival, *Fontana, California*

"The most important thing is what your thoughts are after you've done something wrong. If you can rehash it, re-visualize it, and make it happen the way you want it to happen, then you're ready for the next ground ball. It is very essential that you don't think something negative, because that carries on to something worse."

Alex Rodriguez, *New York, New York*

"No matter how many times you say, 'It's over, I got to move on,' you're still thinking about it. I just put positive reinforcement in my head like, 'I've caught thousands of groundballs, I'm going to get the next one. I'm not going to miss the next one just because I missed the last one. I know I can catch it.'"
Richie Sexson, *Portland, Oregon*

"Going through (adversity) as a kid, my parents made me understand that only God is perfect. When you take that into anything you do, you play the game and have fun. You don't play scared or with the fear you're going to make a mistake. You just play and what happens, happens. When you pick up the next one and make a good play, your teammates respect you because they know that error didn't beat you mentally."
Gary Sheffield, *Tampa, Florida*

"People say they want the next ball hit to them. As a kid you say, 'If I get another one, I might make an error.' You need to reverse that thought and say, 'All right, if the next ball is hit to me, I'm going to make the play.' That's something even professionals go through. I visualize the ball coming toward me and making the play. I visualize catching it and throwing it. You want to focus on the good and recreate the muscle memory and those good habits. If you create those good habits, they're more likely to continue to happen."
Mark Teixeira, *Severna Park, Maryland*

TAKING STEPS

"I visualize the ball coming toward me and making a play. You want to focus on the good."

—MARK TEIXEIRA

"Tino Martinez (ML career, 1990-2005) told me when he's in a slump, each day makes him that much closer to coming out of it. Instead of thinking how far down you're going, I'm bound to come out of this very soon. Look at what's positive."

Jason Veritek, *Rochester, Michigan*

"Once you've given up the home run or you've walked the guy, you can't take it back. All you can do is work on the next guy. Getting too excited or trying to overdo it tends to get people in trouble rather than trusting whatever it was that was getting guys out on the previous pitches is the same thing that's going to get the next guy out. Just knowing that 70 percent of the time they're going to get out even if they're a good hitter. You have to find positive things to draw from. Say things that are going to produce productivity and not negativity. You got to stay positive and continue to convince yourself that if you execute what you're trying to do, more often then not, you're going to have success."

Kip Wells, *Houston, Texas*

TAKING STEPS

"Say things that are going to produce productivity and not negativity."

—KIP WELLS

"I just tell myself over and over again, 'You'll get the next one.' I don't reflect upon myself as a poor player, just a player that had a poor performance. I always try to talk positively to myself and my teammates. If you're a positive person and you're generally a happy person, people pick up on that."

Gregg Zaun, *Glendale, California.*

Step up to the challenge:

- Which big leaguer's advice on dealing with the "Error Monster" are you going to try the next time you make an error or mistake?
- What encouraging words would you like to hear from your teammates or coaches right after you made an error?
- What have you discovered about yourself when you've come out of a slump?

Step out of the box to look for the signs

Try this for a week: As you go about your day, start to notice what you say to yourself when you make a mistake. Imagine if you were a Major Leaguer, what would you say to a young ballplayer to help them move past a mistake or slump?

CHAPTER 5

Success Secrets
To The Game

*"Watch people that are successful
and try to emulate them."*

—BOB FELLER

When someone tells you a secret, they're letting you into their private treasure chest of knowledge and information that perhaps only a few know about. And that information can be valuable to those who are willing to listen and use it.

Players share secrets and informational tips with each other all the time. They want to learn as much as they can about the other team so they can be successful when playing against them. The more information you gather to educate yourself, the greater your advantage. It's like being in charge of your own all-star team—you feel more confident about your options and choices.

Great information doesn't have to be a secret. It can come in the form of a book you read or advice you hear from a teacher, parent or friend. No matter where the information comes from, it's there to help you improve your skills and become a better player and person.

In the following pages, you have access to valuable information and tips on what it takes for these Big Leaguers to be successful, overcome challenges and stay on top of their game. As you read this chapter, look for ways to apply these success secrets to all areas of your life.

"Chris Bando was my manager in Double-A (minor league). The best advice he ever gave me was a little acronym called: ACE—Attitude. Concentration. Effort. He said that those are the things you can control every game. Prepare yourself, and keep a consistent attitude of putting others before yourself. Concentrate on your game plan and give it your best effort."

Josh Bard, *Ithaca, New York*

"K.I.S.S. Keep It Simple Stupid. It's a very difficult game. You got to have a thought. You got to have a plan. You got to have an idea. The simpler you keep it, the easier the game is going to be. But you still got to have an idea of what you want to do."

Craig Biggio, *Smithtown, New York*

"Never accept losing, but learn to deal with losing. If you accept losing, then everything in your life you'll accept if it goes bad. You have to learn how to deal with adversity. If you can't deal with it, whether you play baseball, or a doctor or a teacher, you're going to have a tough go in life."

Larry Bowa, *Sacramento, California*

TAKING STEPS

"It doesn't take any talent to hustle."

—SEAN CASEY

"It doesn't take any talent to hustle. It doesn't matter how good you are, it doesn't take any talent to play the game right, to play the game hard. My dad was really big on that."

Sean Casey, *Willingboro, New Jersey*

"I'll play the game in my head before I actually play it on the field. I'll mentally go over or visualize what (the pitcher's) going to pitch to me. I try to play everything in my head before hand. It makes you very prepared."

Jeff Conine, *Tacoma, Washington*

"Continue to make adjustments every day, keep learning and pay attention. It's like going to school. If you want to be a better student, you have to pay attention in class. We were playing the Angels and I just watched Garret Anderson take batting practice trying to pick up as much information as possible."

Carl Crawford, *Houston, Texas*

"I don't like to fail. That's one thing I have yet to learn about this game. You have to fail to be successful. How you handle it on the field dictates how well you're going to do and how well you're going to carry on in life."

Adam Dunn, *Houston, Texas*

"I asked Alan Trammel (ML career, 1977-1996) how he was able to be so consistent for so long. He said that good day or bad day, he makes sure he follows his routine. He stays focused on the things that create the result, not the result—the process. I've always taken that to heart; to make sure on and off the field, I do things I believe in that are right and are going to make me a complete person."

Damion Easley, *New York, New York*

"Bruce Sutter lived down the street from me (ML career, 1976-1988; HOF, 2006). He always told me, 'Play hard every day and don't sell yourself short.' I try to play hard every day and not try to do too much. I don't try to be somebody I'm not, but go out there and be Adam."

Adam Everett, *Austell, Georgia*

"Watch the people that are successful, the best in their business, and try to emulate them as best you can."

Bob Feller, *Van Meter, Iowa Hall of Fame, 1962*

"I try to go out and have fun and not make it a lifeand-death situation. This is just a game. Yes, everybody wants to win, but somebody has to lose also. Losing is part of the game and it builds character too. When it's a tough situation, I know I've been there before and have the ability to get out of it. I try not to get too caught up in the moment. I try to maintain my concentration level and make good, quality pitches to get out of the situation."

John Franco, *Brooklyn, New York*

"Have fun and play hard. Those are the two qualities that have nothing to do with physical ability or physical talent. You can always have fun and you can always play hard."

Troy Glaus, *Tarzana, California*

"My dad was the person I wanted to be like growing up. He said, 'You're not me. Don't imitate anybody. Just be yourself.' Go out there and have some fun and be true to yourself."

Ken Griffey Jr., *Donora, Pennsylvania*

"Just be a professional and carry yourself the right way. You have to realize that everybody is watching everything you do. If you handle yourself the right way then things will be fine."

Toby Hall, *Tacoma, Washington*

"Everybody told me when I was young, 'You need to play the game smart and follow the rules.' Play the game like a professional. When you play like a professional you're going to get better and that's the most important thing."

Livan Hernandez, *Villa Clara, Cuba*

"You got to be a good listener in this game if you want to be a good player. There's a lot of people out there who want to help, but at the same time there are a lot of players that want you to do bad. You have to pick the right people to listen to and go from there. You got

TAKING STEPS

"You have to pick the right people to listen to."

—RAMON HERNANDEZ

to learn from the older players and the coaches because they've been playing more than you."

Ramon Hernandez, *Caracas, Venezuela*

"Two words, 'What if?' Never leave yourself with the question, 'What if?' What if I had tried a little harder? What if I had spent a little more time studying at school or studying my craft? It's pretty simple. What if I had gotten along better with others? What if I had respected my parents a little more? It's pretty important stuff."

Trevor Hoffman, *Bellflower, California*

"Lots of times a player says bad things when a team releases him. They don't realize that baseball's a small fraternity. The next team you try out for will call the General Manager that just released you and ask, 'What kind of guy was he? How did he leave your team?' And the General Manager says, 'He didn't know how to handle himself.' If there's somebody who's just as talented as you, they'll take the guy with a better attitude."

Rex Hudler, *Tempe, Arizona*

"My parents told me, 'No matter how far you may get in this game, you're still no better than nobody else. The Lord blessed you with this talent to play this game, you keep your head level.'"

Orlando Hudson, *Darlington, South Carolina*

"Kirby Puckett (ML career, 1984-1995; HOF, 2001) and Dave Winfield (ML career, 1973-1995; HOF, 2001) always said, 'It's going to be a long journey. Be patient.' Patience is the key. A lot of people want (success) fast. That's what I wanted as a young guy. It's not going to work out when you want it, but it'll be there. You will be rewarded. You have to go through struggle to have progress. That's what I did and most of these players did."

Torii Hunter, *Pine Bluff, Arkansas*

"Know what you need to do when you go out there and give 100 percent even if you don't feel 100 percent. Do the best you can to help your team win."

Andruw Jones, *Willemstad, Curacao*

"You try to go into the game with as much knowledge as you can so you're prepared, just like a test in school. If you study of a bunch, you feel better about taking the test because you know you prepared. That way there are no surprises. You look at what the other pitchers are throwing. You pay attention to what's going on when you're not playing or involved because that's when you can learn the most."

Paul Konerko, *Providence, Rhode Island*

TAKING STEPS

"You have to put a legitimate effort into anything that's important."

—TONY LA RUSSA

"Tony Perez (ML career, 1964-1986; HOF, 2000) was extremely instrumental in my early playing career. He told me to keep my eyes and ears open and my mouth closed. He told me I could learn a lot by watching. I try to learn from my mistakes and from the mistakes of others I see around me. I try not to make the same mistakes as them."

Barry Larkin, *Cincinnati, Ohio*

"You have to put a legitimate effort into anything that's important, whether it's your family life, education, friends, or relationships. Nobody really does well in this game, or in life off the field, unless they're willing to work."

Tony La Russa, *Tampa, Florida*

"Baseball teaches you discipline, how to recover from negative things and how to work together to achieve a goal. It teaches you to understand that life isn't always good things. There are times you're going to struggle and working hard is important. The amount of work you put in, repays you. If you have the ability and the drive, you'd be shortchanging yourself if you didn't maximize your talent."

Mike Lowell, *San Juan, Puerto Rico*

"Billy Connors asked me around my second or third year, 'You ever wonder how good you could be at this game?' I guess he kind of challenged me to go find out."

Greg Maddux, *San Angelo, Texas*

"My parents told me if I got on a team, there was no quitting or not showing up for a practice when something else was more convenient. I learned a lot of lessons about commitment, teamwork, sticking through tough times, and overcoming some obstacles. I learned about trusting other people and how hard you can push yourself in training. There's so many lessons kids can learn that won't only make them better baseball players, but make them successful in every walk of life."

Mike Matheny, *Columbus, Ohio*

"Baseball is 90 percent mental and 10 percent physical. If you program your mind before you do something, you can do anything you want. It's a discipline. Not too many people have the ability to play this sport. They have a weak mind and they quit right away and say, 'I can't handle this anymore!' You need to have a strong mind."

Melvin Mora, *Aguas Negras,*
Venezuela

TAKING STEPS

*"When you work hard ...
and spill your guts out there,
good things will happen."*
—TROT NIXON

"You never know who's watching. Always conduct your business in a knowledgeable and professional way. I was playing right field in a legion game one day. I was usually at shortstop. So I was hustling out to right field and hustling in. A guy came to see me play and wondered why I wasn't at shortstop. But he understood the type of make up I had by taking on another position, hustling and going about my business in a mature way. It helped me to get a scholarship to go to school and it gave me an opportunity to play some more baseball and get an education."

Bill Mueller, *Maryland Heights, Missouri*

"Don't cheat your fans. Don't cheat yourself. When you work hard for something and spill your guts out there, good things will happen. You should have no worries if things don't go your way."

Trot Nixon, *Durham, North Carolina*

"Desire. One guy might have all the tools, but he doesn't show that he wants to be the best out there. A lot of times I might not be the best, but I'm striving to be the best.

Even the superstar says, "I can be better," where another guy says, 'I'm as good as I can be.' "

Buck O'Neil, *Carrabelle, Florida*

"Baseball's a game where you have to learn to deal with failure. You have to learn from your mistakes and try to make yourself better in baseball as you would in life. It builds character when you make it through tough times. When you get angry on the field, it doesn't make you any better to show it. Take some deep breaths to regain your focus or your thoughts."

Dean Palmer, *Tallahassee, Florida*

"Never give up. There are going to be hard times and you're going to lose, but learn from the hard times and from losing games. But believe the hard times will make you stronger and smarter to be a winner. Don't give up and don't forget your dream and just keep doing and trying."

Chan Ho Park, *Kongju, South Korea*

"This is a sport you got to stay really disciplined every day. It's a long season. You got to be disciplined on making sure you get your work in. That's what it has taught me in life, staying disciplined in the classroom, with money or having discipline in your faith, going to church."

Mark Prior, *San Diego, California*

TAKING STEPS

*"Focus and put your priorities
in order, and you deal with
one thing at a time."*

—GARY SHEFFIELD

"There are a lot of guys I played with growing up that were better baseball players than I was that didn't make it to the big leagues. It's a matter of work ethic. Learning to play the game right and being a team player is very important. Doing the little things right; bunting, fielding, or being a student of the game. That's helped me get to where I am and not just sheer ability."

Dave Roberts, *Okinawa, Japan*

"Have your eyes and ears open and your mouth shut. The game unfolds itself, if you just pay attention. If you're not shooting your mouth off trying to be seen and noticed, rather you notice what's going on around you, you can become a better ball player and a better person."

Scott Rolen, *Evansville, Indiana*

"Tough times don't last, tough people do. My dad told me that when I was a kid and it's something I've never forgotten."

Curt Schilling, *Anchorage, Alaska*

"You have to put your priorities in order. You can easily be thinking of things going on off the field that are affecting you. You focus and put your priorities in order, and you deal with one thing at a time. All your problems are not going to go way trying to get rid of ten of them at a time. (Just like a batting order), you get to it one at a time."

Gary Sheffield, *Tampa, Florida*

"This is not a game of just being on top all the time. You're going to get knocked down. This game has taught me through trials to never give up, overcome injuries, bad outings or what people think of you. It's knowing who I am as a person first and not be consumed as a baseball player with this job or everything this game does to me."

John Smoltz, *Detroit, Michigan*

"I learned a lot from Robin Yount (ML career, 1974-1993; HOF, 1999) when I first got to the big leagues. He said, 'You're not always going to do the right thing every day, but you should be trying to do the right thing.'"

B. J. Surhoff, *Bronx, New York*

"It's not what you do when you walk in the door, it's what you do when you leave. It's the lasting impressions you give and how you handle the bad times. It's very similar to life. It's all about understanding, making adjustments and having responsibility for everything you do. My parents, family and my wife were a big influence."

Jim Thome, *Peoria, Illinois*

"Never give up no matter what other people say or think about you. If you really believe in yourself, you can accomplish a lot of things. In this game you have a lot of people telling you that you can't play, you're too small, or don't have a strong enough arm. You have to forget that and really push yourself and believe that you belong here."

Omar Vizquel, *Caracas, Venezuela*

"Never forget where you came from. A minor-league director I had painted a picture for me of a turtle on a fence post. (The turtle) had help getting up the fence post. Through your career there's been a lot of people to help you get to where you are and help you be successful."

Tim Wakefield, *Melbourne, Florida*

"I came from a real small town (Webster, Wisconsin). I always told people I was going to play in the major leagues and people always said, 'Okay, keep going to school, too.' But I proved a lot of people wrong. Where

---

TAKING STEPS

"Never give up no matter what other people say or think about you."

—OMAR VIZQUEL

I come from, nobody gets to make it big. Baseball's taught me I can do anything I put my mind to."

Jarrod Washburn, *LaCrosse, Wisconsin*

"You're doing yourself a disservice by not paying attention as a pitcher, 'What did I do this outing good and what did I do this outing poorly? What do I need to try to concentrate on next time out?' You find out a lot about yourself by putting yourself in a situation to be successful. Maybe you're not in the game, but you're prepared that one time you get in. Guys put themselves in situations to be successful, but it's only because of hard work and preparation that those things come out in your favor."

Kip Wells, *Houston, Texas*

"(Early in my career) I was tasting success. Willie Randolph (ML career, 1975-1992) told me, 'Don't be afraid of success. Don't think this is a fluke or think you're not going to be able to do this over and over again, because you won't if you think that way. Have confidence in your ability to play and be used to that. You can't think that at some point you're going to fail and you are not going to be able to do it anymore.' "

Bernie Williams, *San Juan, Puerto Rico*

"A lot of people say, 'Keep your head up, no matter what you go through, good or bad.' Just as in life, you're going to go through adversity. That's just something I learned in life from losing a lot of big games. It teaches you class."

Dontrelle Willis, *Alameda, California*

"To keep myself mentally prepared for the game, I remembered the lean years. I'd think about those days (living) in the projects with my eight sisters four brothers and five of us in a bed. (I thought about) making 20-hour bus trips, getting a $1.25 a day meal money, not eating with my teammates playing in the south, and staying in a different hotel. I thought about making $150 a month my first year and married with two children. By focusing on those things kept me hungry. I never got content. I did not play baseball. I worked baseball."

Maury Wills, *Washington, DC*

"Mentally you have to have confidence in yourself, stay positive and know you belong in this league. If you have doubt, it's going to linger and you're going to say to yourself, 'See I told you so.' My rookie year I made eight errors in the first month and I got sent down to AAA. I could've easily shut down and said, 'That's it for my career.' But I went down and I worked on things, stayed positive and starting having fun again. The next thing I know I'm back up here a few weeks later. Getting sent down from the Major Leagues is a pretty big thing and tough to take. But you're still playing baseball and still got a job and that's the main thing."

Jack Wilson, *West Lake Village, California*

"You learn how to deal with adversity and keep going. Life is about adversity, problems and overcoming them. That's kind of what baseball is. Even when you're good,

TAKING STEPS

"You're the only one that can tell you that you can't do it.

—GREG ZAUN

you fail a lot. And if you know how to handle that, you'll be pretty good in life."

Dave Winfield, *St. Paul, Minnesota Hall of Fame, 2001*

"Always remember what your strengths are and how you got to this position. Focus on those things and don't let people try to get you to do things you're not capable of doing. Too often when people begin to struggle, we as coaches like to change them. You have to look back and figure out what got that person to where they are. Then work on those things and make those things better, rather then try to change someone to do something they're not capable of doing."

Robin Yount, *Danville, Illinois Hall of Fame, 1999*

"You have set goals for yourself, however small and never give up. You're the only one that can tell you that you can't do it. If you have the attitude you can succeed and nobody's going to stop you, more often than not you'll be successful."

Gregg Zaun, *Glendale, California*

Step up to the challenge:

- Which player's success secrets do you think will best help you in baseball? In school? At home? With your friends?
- Which success secrets have you heard before that didn't come from a baseball player? From where did they come?
- What's the secret to YOUR success?

Step out of the box to look for the signs

Try this for a week: As you go about your day, start to notice other people's success. Ask them what their secret is to success. What are some of the things they do to be successful and how can you bring it into your life?

CHAPTER 6

Signs of A Champion

*"You become a champion first, mentally,
then the championship comes."*

—ALEX RODRIGUEZ

A s you probably know in baseball, the team to score the most runs in the game wins. The Most Valuable Player Award is given to the best player in each league. What if we never kept score? How would you know who the winner was? If they never handed out trophies, who would be the champion?

The point is: How could you tell if a person was a "winner" in a sport with which you aren't familiar?

Do you think you could recognize if a person was a champion just by the way they walked down the street? I believe you could.

Champions definitely do things differently to set themselves apart from the rest. They work smarter and harder at becoming better at what they do. In their mind, they see and think of themselves in a certain way. Did you know the way you think and feel about yourself has a huge impact on how well you're able to do something or rebound from a setback? When your brain is pumping in bad or negative stuff in your head, it's tough to have great things happen.

Watch a champion and see how they learn from their mistakes. Instead of getting down on themselves, champions look at an error as an opportunity to get better. They realize that there's more game to be played.

It's like when you take a test in school and you get a question wrong. You can't dwell on the one you got wrong; there are more questions on the test.

At any given time there are at least 750 baseball players in the world playing Major League Baseball. The players I talked with shared their thoughts on what it takes to be and feel like a champion at this high level. Read on to find out what they say are the signs of a champion. It may surprise you.

"A champion is a guy who makes people around him better. Just by being yourself, people sort of migrate to people who are leaders. He's a guy who plays through pain and never quits, no matter how bad things go. If you believe in yourself, you stay with that goal."

Larry Bowa, *Sacramento, California*

"He is selfless, works hard, self-motivated and has passion for what he does. He's always looking to get better, always listening for advice. He's not thinking that he knows everything. He's a winner. He doesn't make excuses. He takes responsibility for his actions."

Sean Casey, *Willingboro, New Jersey*

"You have to have a lot of ambition. You have to be mentally tough and have the desire to be the best player you can be and want to win. You have to hate losing with a passion, but be a good sportsman too."

Carl Crawford, *Houston, Texas*

"He's a clutch player and has the mentality of always wanting to win. He's always thinking the right way like, 'I'm going to get a hit. I'm going to do this. I'm going to steal this base.' It's never, 'I'm not going to strike out.' Or 'I hope I do this.' A champion always gives off an air about himself. (It's a leadership) mentality, always picking up the other guys, patting everybody on the back and you can feel that."

Coco Crisp, *Los Angeles, California*

TAKING STEPS

"A champion has good work habits and is not afraid to ask questions."

—JOHN FRANCO

"A champion just figures out a way to get things done no matter what. They just figure out a way to win."
Morgan Ensberg, *Redondo Beach, California*

"A champion has good work habits and is not afraid to ask questions. Look at the veteran guys—at how they carry themselves and how they approach situations. I was fortunate. When I came up with Cincinnati, one of the top relief pitchers at the time was Tom Hume (ML career, 1977-1987). I learned how to carry myself on and off the field."
John Franco, *Brooklyn, New York*

"It all comes back to preparation before the game, doing your normal routine. During the game, thinking of situations where you know where to throw the ball if it's hit to you. That's all a part of mental preparation. That'll get you through the times when you're a little sluggish."
Brian Giles, *El Cajon, California*

"Certain traits can increase your chances of winning because you have a championship attitude. It has a lot to do with your character. What good is it if you're winning a championship and you cheated to get there? That's not a champion. A champion has respect for others, the game and values other people's feelings. It's a lot deeper than just winning something."
Doug Glanville, *Hackensack, New Jersey*

"I do some visualization. I sit in a quiet place before or during the game. I'll go through an at-bat or a play on the field where I'm succeeding. Another thing I do is pay attention to the game. Probably two-thirds of the guys even at this level don't really pay attention to see what the pitcher is trying to do. If you really pay attention, you see things that are so obvious. I'll watch how pitchers want to get a hitter out when it's a crucial time and see what pitches they really rely on."
Shawn Green, *Des Plaines, Illinois*

"Nowadays people aren't really judged about what's inside their heart or mind, it's all about wins or losses. And I understand that being a part of the playing field at this level. But the mark of a true champion is someone that's willing to stick their neck out and stand for the right thing and lead."
Trevor Hoffman, *Bellflower, California*

"Champion's (have) attitudes that are different than the guys who (don't). You've heard the phrase of somebody

TAKING STEPS

"A champion (goes) beyond what he thought he could do."

—RANDY JOHNSON

being a winner and somebody not being a winner. The qualities they possess are just different. You can see that. It's their attitude—positive attitude. Their personality is outgoing. They're not really concerned with themselves as much as their team."

Tim Hudson, *Columbus, Georgia*

"A champion understands what he's playing for and what he wants to achieve. He's willing to give it his all and go beyond what he thought he could do."

Randy Johnson, *Walnut Creek, California*

"My senior quote coming out of high school was, 'When God measures a man, He puts a tape around his heart, not his head.' Having heart allows you to persevere through all the (adversity) you'll go through, not only in your career but in life. That was one thing that my dad told me that's always stuck with me. If you just have that inner desire to persevere, then things eventually will come out on the positive side."

Chipper Jones, *DeLand, Florida*

"A champion is someone who's not afraid to fail. Someone who wanted the opportunity. The greatest thing in life is to get an opportunity and to take advantage of it. That is all anybody should ever ask for. Nothing should ever be given to them, but you should always want the opportunity. Whether you fail, which is not the most important thing, you want to be in that position. You want to be the one who is up there last of the ninth inning and you have to have a base hit. Or be the guy who's going to get the next hitter out to win the World Series."

Al Kaline, *Baltimore, Maryland Hall of Fame, 1980*

"He is not scared. He's not going to back down from a challenge, especially when he's not doing well. 'Champion' doesn't always mean that he's the winner. It's a guy who knows what his job is, comes to do it every day and plays hard all the time. He's totally focused on what he's doing all the time and gives to his teammates."

Paul Konerko, *Providence, Rhode Island*

"I'm a big believer of imagery. At home, I'll play the day through before it happens, so when it happens, I'm not surprised. I'm prepared for it. You see your ride to the ballpark. You see yourself getting dressed (and) starting your routine. Everything just falls into place. I believe in setting goals and having a strong routine that you're not going to deviate from."

Joe McEwing, *Bristol, Pennsylvania*

"Someone with a great mind, a person who's quiet. He knows he's the best. He doesn't say it. A guy who's humble, that's a champion to me, not the guy who's always talking about it and saying things about himself."
Bengie Molina, *Rio Piedras, Puerto Rico*

"I can be very stubborn both positive and negative ways. When I was young, I wanted so badly to perform well and the harder I worked, the better I thought I would be. I wasn't always open to suggestions on how to play the game, to a fault. That stubbornness probably held me back as a young player. When I got into pro baseball, I realized there are a lot of guys with a lot of experience and a whole lot better than I am. If I was going to get anywhere, I was going to have to open up more, take their advice and apply it, trial and error. I took that stubbornness of trying to do it all myself to a stubbornness of paying attention to details."
Terry Mulholland, *Uniontown, Pennsylvania*

"You don't have to have great stuff. If you have a big heart and you're willing to put in the work, you can will your way to get some stuff done. I've been able to pitch up here with a lot of heart whenever I wasn't able to throw a hard fastball or have a great curveball that night. It's made me a stronger man dealing with a lot of adversity."
Andy Pettitte, *Baton Rouge, Louisiana*

"Trust in your ability. You can talk yourself into or out of almost any situation. You can talk yourself into winning when you don't think you have the ability to win and you can talk yourself into losing when you do have the ability to win and be successful. So much of it is how you perceive yourself. If you like yourself and respect yourself, you can look yourself in the mirror and answer the questions, 'Have I worked as hard as I can, have I prepared myself as well as I can?' Confidence and trust go with that."

Bryan Price, *San Francisco, California*

'I write underneath the bill of my cap, 'One who can persevere through difficult times.' It's someone who can look in the face of the impossible and say, 'You know what? I'm going to get through this.' That ties into life, not just in baseball. I've had two major elbow operations. I had a buddy in the hospital at the same time (as my surgery) who was going through leukemia. He was getting a bone marrow transplant. It threw me back in the direction of faith and purpose in life. I get a card from him that said, 'Encouragement'. The inside dealt with perseverance. Through his words he told me

TAKING STEPS

"A champion is not afraid to make mistakes."

—JIMMY ROLLINS

to hang in there and things would be okay. Here's a guy in the hospital fighting for his life, sending me a card and I was feeling sorry for myself. He was my hero, my champion. Today he's married and has two beautiful daughters. That's a champion, one who can persevere."

Nate Robertson, *Wichita, Kansas*

"A champion is complete, determined, resilient and nonstop. It's all about being resilient and building to be a champion. You become a champion first mentally, with everything you do, and then the championship comes. It's not the other way around."

Alex Rodriguez, *New York, New York*

"A champion is not afraid to make mistakes. Some people are very tentative and afraid of success. Well, you're going to have problems if you're poor, you're going to have problems if you're rich. You're going to have problems if you are successful or unsuccessful. So you might as well be the best you can be and see where that takes you. If you make a mistake, learn from it and keep on ticking."

Jimmy Rollins, *Oakland California*

"It's the guys that work hard, don't give up, believe in themselves, and make other people all around them better. Anybody can play this game when it's going good. How do you play when things are going bad? What kind of person are you? That's the key in anything in life."

Tim Salmon, *Long Beach, California*

"Determination and will are the signs of a champion. It's something within you. You can reach down inside and get it. If I am determined to get something done, I'm going to get it done!"

Gary Sheffield, *Tampa, Florida*

"First of all, you have to dream. You have to think big and have a different picture. A champion is a leader whose view is always different. A Champion strives every day, no matter what the perks are, to be his best. There's no motivation other than selfmotivation. It's the desire to be the best and one that perseveres."

John Smoltz, *Detroit, Michigan*

"If you give 100 percent every time you step on the field, and you have done everything you can to prepare yourself, if you do that enough times, you're going to be a champion not only in baseball, but in life probably. Baseball prepares you for so many things. If you're playing and competing as hard as you can, then at the end of the day, you have no reason to hang your head."

J. T. Snow, *Long Beach, California*

"(Being a champion) has more to do than talent—it's a belief system. Four or five years ago, I knew I could be a major-league pitcher but I didn't believe it. That next year, I believed. I had some success and I believed I was a major league pitcher. The second that you believe

TAKING STEPS

*"... it's what you do after you fail
(that) makes champions champions."*
—SCOTT SULLIVAN

that you belong up here is the same time you're going to have success."
Justin Speier, *Walnut Creek, California*

"It's the ultimate desire to do what it takes to win a ballgame—the sacrifice, the hard work, the perseverance. Everybody goes through failures. It's not the fact that you fail, it's what you do after you fail (that) makes champions champions."
Scott Sullivan, *Tuscaloosa, Alabama*

"Win or lose, a champion stands up for his actions. If you lose the game, you don't throw an excuse out. Stand and face it. If you win the game, do the same. A champion really won't take the credit for it nine times out of 10. They'll give that away. They'll spread the wealth and face the blame."
Mike Timlin, *Midland, Texas*

"Determination is probably most important. You have to be confident. You also have to be humble (and have respect) at the same time."
Chase Utley, *Pasadena, California*

TAKING STEPS

"If you don't believe what you have, talent means nothing."

—FERNANDO VALENZUELA

"To be successful in this game, you have to believe in yourself. The talent is there, but if you don't believe what you have, talent means nothing. The main thing is to believe in yourself."

Fernando Valenzuela, *Navojoa, Mexico*

"A champion has a toughness of the mind and body. You got to have perseverance and the ability to make adjustments. You got to have pride in yourself to make sure that this is an important thing for you. You just can't throw yourself out there and expect to be successful. You got to do your work."

Bernie Williams, *San Juan, Puerto Rico*

"Someone who is willing to sacrifice anything to get the job done. When I see champion, I see passion, desire, and an incredible competitive fire."

Michael Young, *Covina, California*

"It's a guy who's not afraid to be different, scrutinized, or made fun of. All the true champions in life are basically different. They try things that have never been tried.

They say, 'This has never happened, so I'm still going to give it my best shot.' Whereas everyone else will say, 'That's never happened so it's never going happen.' They have a strong belief in what they're doing and they see it in their mind. They're thinking outside the box and it takes a lot courage to do those things."

Barry Zito, *Las Vegas, Nevada*

Step up to the challenge:

- Which player's approach to being a champion did you like the best?
- How do you show up as a champion at school? At home? With your friends?
- What are some steps a champion can take to come back from a poor performance?

Step out of the box to look for the signs

Try this for a week: As you go about your day, start to notice the different signs or qualities of a champion in people you know. What makes them a champion? Is it their actions, words, follow through or attitude? How can you conduct yourself in a similar manner?

CHAPTER

What the Game Has Taught Me ...

*"... to be a complete person;
to learn from success and struggle."*

—DONTRELLE WILLIS

There's nothing like the excitement of an extra inning ball game. During extra inning games and big games the intensity is higher and every pitch, at-bat or out is crucial to the outcome of the game. Those moments not only define memorable games, but they can define players and build character.

So to add a little excitement, I included an extra chapter, Bonus Baseball! And just like an extra inning game, this bonus chapter really encapsulates the theme of the book.

Players are used to talking about what it takes to achieve success, overcome adversity, and battle through injuries and so on.

I wanted to go deeper. I wanted to know, drawing from their experiences from the first time they ever put on a baseball uniform to today, how the game has truly impacted these big-time players? How have all those lesson carried over into life both on and off the field?

It was a challenging question for many players to answer. Perhaps they were used to a lot of "fastball" questions, and my "curveball" question took them by surprise!

I'm glad it did because they took the question seriously. They paused, thought, and really searched for their answer. Their first response was, "Wow, no one's ever asked me that question before."

In this chapter you'll get to read a different side of these big-time ball players that you may not have seen before. It's a more personal and human side where they really reveal what they've learned about themselves from playing baseball. Their honest and insightful answers may surprise you; it did to many of them!

"It's taught me I am mentally tougher than a lot of other people. I played against guys with a lot more talent and never made it. I can see six or seven surgeries, a couple of them career threatening, and I'm still hanging around playing good. I know myself a little bit more."

Moises Alou, *Atlanta, Georgia*

"It's taught me competition is important. It's something that can teach a lot about life. It's a game, though it's not the most important thing, it's okay when you're playing to make it the most important thing and give it everything you have."

David Bell, *Cincinnati, Ohio*

"I learned in order to play this game I really got to prepare myself. Every year goes by I have to work harder. I can't sit back on my skills. I got to perform, execute and keep improving and think positive."

Carlos Beltran, *Manati, Puerto Rico*

"I've had some great moments with the game and some pretty big disappointments and failures. In that way it mirrors life and helps you deal with things. I appreciate and am thankful when things are going well, and when they're not, I'm mentally tough enough to battle through the hard times. That's one of the big benefits I've gotten from playing baseball. Hard work is rewarded. My dad always told me that if you want to be really good at something, you have to be willing to pay the price."

Lance Berkman, *Waco, Texas*

"It taught me to not take things for granted. I played 15 years in the big leagues and made six All-Star teams. But I went to every spring training with the idea I had to win a job. After three or four years I could've very easily said, 'You know what? This job is mine.' You have to work. You can't take shortcuts in life to get where you want to go. It just doesn't happen."

Larry Bowa, *Sacramento, California*

"It's taught me perseverance. I've been able to deal with other things in my life that were going on. It was like my whole world was crumbling before my eyes. Sometimes I didn't want to come back to play baseball ever again. But you shrug it off and come back the next day and get after it."

Eric Chavez, *Los Angeles, California*

"It's taught me how to get along with people. You meet so many different people from different areas and different aspects of life. It's allowed me to become a better communicator and a better teammate. It's taught me how to appreciate the things I have and work ethic. In order to succeed in anything in life you have to have work ethic."

Michael Cuddyer, *Norfolk, Virginia*

"It's taught me about the mental strength you have to have in yourself. There are so many ups and downs in this game. All the pressure and trials in your life really

develop your personality and the way you accept things. You got thousands people every night wanting you to drive in the winning run and sometimes you strike out. You have to learn to handle the ups and downs of life and it's personified in a baseball game."
Rick Dempsey, *Fayetteville, Tennessee*

"I've learned whether you're struggling or playing well, you learn a lot about what type of person you are."
Jermaine Dye, *Oakland, California*

"You really learn how to face the fears you have and stand up in front of a lot of people. You're vulnerable because everybody knows you messed up. Just being able to stand up there and accept (it), you're not going to be happy with it, but being able to cope with it, makes me feel very good that I'm able to do that."
Morgan Ensberg, *Redondo Beach, California*

TAKING STEPS

"You really learn how to face the fears you have."

—MORGAN ENSBERG

"The hardest person to know is yourself. To know yourself is very important. Your character is like your shadow. Once you establish your character, it will be with you forever. That's one of the things baseball and the military has taught me about myself."

Bob Feller, *Van Meter, Iowa Hall of Fame, 1962*

"It's taught me that I'm a stronger person than I think I am. Sometimes when I feel like I can't do something or I feel insignificant, when I was younger, there was always something I was able to excel at to give myself self-praise I needed to make me feel important."

Brian Fuentes, *Merced, California*

"It's taught me about discipline, being on time, being prepared and how important that is in all aspects of life. The importance of hard work, accountability and responsibility. You need those same qualities to be a good student. We all want to be successful at what we do. In this game you fail a lot. It teaches you how to fail. And what do you do with that failure? Does it freeze you or motivate you?"

Joe Girardi, *Peoria, Illinois*

"It's taught me about keeping a positive attitude when you have really bad stretches and when you're doing extremely well to stay grounded. It's helped me keep a balance between success and failure."

Khalil Greene, *Butler, Pennsylvania*

"You're not as good as they say you are and you're not as bad as you think you are. That's the bottom line!"
Ken Griffey Jr., *Donora, Pennsylvania*

"I always felt like I could do anything I wanted to do, whether it be in school or sports. I don't know if it was something my parents told me, or how I was brought up, but I always felt that way. Baseball has just basically proven if I work hard enough at anything and care about something as bad as I care about the game, I can do it."
Todd Helton, *Knoxville, Tennessee*

"Baseball has made me a grown man. I came to this country when I was 17 years old speaking no English and I got to deal with it. All I did was listen to people. I knew I had to learn English because I had no choice. I had to (take care of) myself and my family."
Ramon Hernandez, *Caracas, Venezuela*

"(Baseball teaches you about) working hard, responsibility and accountability for your actions. You're going to be accountable for what you do on the field after the game. Sometimes they're good things, sometimes they're bad thing. In life, it's what you do at home. You got to be accountable for your actions. It's no different what you do in life and no different what you do in your profession.
Randy Johnson, *Walnut Creek, California*

TAKING STEPS

"Devote all (your) energy to the stuff that matters."

—PAUL KONERKO

"It's taught me how tough I can be mentally. It teaches you to put your energy toward the things you can control. You only have so much mental energy to burn every day. The guys who do it the best devote all their energy to the stuff that matters and the stuff you can control."

Paul Konerko, *Providence,*
Rhode Island

"To play baseball on an everyday basis you have to be very patient and very strong mentally. It's a game of failure. You have to have a lot of self-confidence; especially when you get out and you still understand you're doing a good job. You just keep moving forward."

Derek Lee, *Sacramento, California*

"It's taught me to be patient. After I got drafted I had four surgeries after four years. It was very difficult. It's helped me be patient with my relationships off the field."

Brad Lidge, *Sacramento, California*

"It's taught me how to deal with adversity. You strike out with the bases loaded. You feel like quitting. Are you going to quit? No. There have been times in my career when a lot of people said I couldn't do certain things. That didn't discourage me. I felt like I believed in myself and could do the job."

Mark Loretta, *Santa Monica, California*

"It's taught me I can do anything I want to do. If your mind and your heart are in it and you map out a plan, it's definitely something you can attain. You just have to set the goals and set your heart to it. The biggest thing is knowing in your heart you're capable of accomplishing what you want."

Gary Matthews Jr., *San Francisco, California*

"You have baseball players that are your idols and you appreciate what they do, sometimes so much that you want to be them. And you realize, just because they are great baseball players doesn't make them great people. I learned at an early age that you can root for your favorite baseball player and appreciate his talent on the field. But when it comes to being a role model, you have your parents to look up to for that."

Lou Merloni, *Framingham, Massachusetts*

"I've learned about myself, that I have good qualities and I have bad qualities. I've had to learn, especially when I was young, about being patient as an athlete.

I was one of those guys who had a little bit of a temper. I had to learn to kind of slow my pace down where I could become more consistent, rather than have too many highs or too many lows. The whole time you're doing that, you're learning about how to deal with other people, about how to respect other people, how to appreciate the opportunities that are given to you along the way."

Paul Molitor, *St. Paul, Minnesota Hall of Fame, 2003*

"It's taught me this game is more mental than physical. I know every time I go through a tough situation, this game gives me the opportunity to come out of it. But you need to keep working. If you take the game for granted then the game will come back and bite you. So you want to be ahead of the game and nothing will take you by surprise. Be good to the game and the game will be good to you."

David Ortiz, *Santo Domingo,*
Dominican Republic

"The biggest thing it's taught me is patience. My patience was terrible, especially as a starting pitcher. I'd just catch the ball, get back on the mound and throw it. I was trying to get the ball to the plate so fast it'd take me out of my game. It taught me to slow down and to take it at its own pace."

Roy Oswalt, *Kosciusko, Mississippi*

"It's taught me I'm never right where I need to be. I've been guilty of (thinking), 'I'm right where I need to be.' That's when you get knocked on your butt. They're a lot of different people trying to give you different perspective. I had a pitching coach I thought I was going to be miserable with. We're very different kind of people. But if I were to take a standpoint of, 'I don't need anything from this guy, I'm right where I need to be. I don't need to gain anything from him.' That would've never have helped me grow as a player."

Nate Robertson, *Wichita, Kansas*

"Baseball goes hand in hand with life: sportsmanship, teamwork, how to work together to accomplish one goal, how to win and lose gracefully. It helps you through the rocky times."

Chad Tracy, *Charlotte, North Carolina*

"Baseball has taught me about the importance of family. What I love most is when I go back home and see my son talking about baseball. There's nothing more special

---

TAKING STEPS

"Baseball has taught me about the importance of family."

—JOSE VIDRO

---

than knowing that my family and mother and father are very proud of what I'm doing."

Jose Vidro, *Mayaguez, Puerto Rico*

"It's taught me (about selfishness). You become very selfish in this game because so much is riding on everybody's performance. My livelihood, my goals and team goals rely on how I play. If I do my job, we may win. So you become very selfish. Playing the game without respect is bad selfishness. For example, a coach asks you to bunt and you say, 'No, I want to hit a home run,' that's bad. If I throw three ground balls or strike out three batters and don't give up any runs and we win the game, that's good selfishness, because I don't want to give up any runs."

Billy Wagner, *Tannersville, Virginia*

"It's taught me perseverance, how to be passionate about something and to keep that desire and focus on trying to be successful. I know a lot of people who are content with being mediocre. With baseball you're always trying to fight to win. A lot of people in life should take that same approach. As you're striving at whatever job you're in, as long as you're trying your best, whether you are successful or not, gives you a lot of confidence that you're able to do something. By focusing on the process, the results will take care of itself."

Tim Wakefield, *Melbourne, Florida*

"It's taught me I should never take anything for granted. That's one of the most important things I've learned about the game and probably the most important thing I've learned in life. Baseball sort of translates to the way you live life. You have to put your work in. Nothing happens magically. If I maintain a consistent approach and make sure I'm doing all the things I need to do on a daily basis, good things are going to happen."

Bernie Williams, *San Juan, Puerto Rico*

"It's taught me how positive I really can be. Going through the minor leagues having some adversity and being (in the Major Leagues) having some adversity, is teaching me to be a complete person; to learn from success and struggle. You just keep the same frame of mind; be positive and smile. Those are traits you take into life. A smile can go a long way."

Dontrelle Willis, *Alameda, California*

"Baseball's taught me about the power of positive thought. Everything in this game is thinking, knowing,

---

TAKING STEPS

"The thoughts we think are basically what happens to us in our life."

—BARRY ZITO

confidence and belief. It's all mental, basically. You got to do the physical things, but baseball's really taught me that day in and day out, the thoughts we think are basically what happens to us in our life."

Barry Zito, *Las Vegas, Nevada.*

Step up to the challenge:

- What have some of your playing experiences taught you about yourself?
- When do you personally feel you've learned the most, after a win or a loss?
- What have you learned on the playing field that has helped you in life off the field, such as at school or at home?

Step out of the box to look for the signs

Try this for a week: As you go about your day, ask yourself what you've learned about yourself after you've done something "successfully" and after you've done something "unsuccessfully."

I hope you've enjoyed this book and got to see a different side of some of your favorite baseball players and what the game has meant to them.

There's a saying, "Baseball is life." Your life isn't just a baseball season; it's all year round. Take advantage of the "home runs" these Major Leaguers have sent your way in this book. Make your experiences on the baseball field work for you off the field, too.

- Be alert and look for the signs.
- Respect your teammates and your opponents.
- Listen to your coaches.
- Play hard, play fair and above all—
- HAVE FUN!

It all starts with a step.

So keep Stepping up to the Plate!

Player Index

About The Author

avid Kloser is a Certified Mental Game Coach, who, "coaches the person inside the player". He helps athletes overcome the need to play perfect, manage their emotions under pressure, and instill confidence to help them be the best player they can be.

As a motivational speaker, David inspires audiences to "step up to the plate" in the game of life. He has spoken to hundreds of organizations, most notably at the baseball Hall of Fame. David currently lives with his wife and daughter in York, Pennsylvania.

If you'd like to book David for your next event, inquire about his mental game coaching, or sign up to receive his FREE weekly "Monday Morning Mental Tips", email david@davidkloser.com.

Autographs

Autographs

Autographs

Autographs

Autographs

Autographs

Made in the USA
Coppell, TX
06 October 2020